There is evidence now that after some progress in racial understanding many Americans have retrogressed to the old black-white polarizations.

Anything then that dispels prejudicial preconceptions ought to be required reading, especially in these days when mutual understanding is such an important commodity for survival.

Author Keith Phillips provides insights into ghetto life—something woefully lacking in the minds of many Christians. The reader is stabbed awake by repeated descriptions of the miasma of despair that characterizes the narrowly circumscribed life of the decaying city.

He furnishes us with a variety of vignettes showing the remarkably changed lives resulting from genuine faith in Christ. It's in these personal word portraits that you can discern the volatile racial tensions which make inner-city evangelistic and mission work so difficult.

To be sure there are culture shocks, for which the readers should be prepared. But those who dare to face them will acquire that good feeling that comes when you have faced a contemporary problem and forged a solution. Phillips' concluding plea is a primer in practicing Christian love.

Billy Graham

EVERYBODY'S AFRAID IN THE GHETTO

EVERYBODY'S AFRAID IN THE GHETTO

by Keith W. Phillips

A Division of G/L Publications
Glendale, California, U.S.A.

*The characters, settings and events in this
narrative are true. To protect the privacy
of the individual, fictitious names and
nicknames are often used.*

Scripture quotations used in this book:
King James Version
NASB, New American Standard Bible. La Habra, CA: The
Lockman Foundation, 1971. Used by permission.
TLB, The Living Bible, Paraphrased. Wheaton:
Tyndale House, Publishers, 1971. Used by permission.

Published by
Regal Books Division, G/L Publications
Glendale, California 91209, U.S.A.

Library of Congress Catalog Card No. 73-87286
ISBN 0-8307-0262-8

CONTENTS

Dr. Vincent Bird FMS gift

FOREWORD

Urban America has sucked up publicity, criticism, fear and interest like a giant vacuum cleaner bent on dominating the domestic scene. A major by-product of the attention generated by the riots, gangs, crime, narcotics and unrest that white America has made synonymous with its inner cities is the belief that the average Caucasian can do little to directly influence the course of events that unfold in the minority dominated urban areas. This mental predisposition has tragically dissuaded most men from any attempt at positive action.

World Impact, Inc. furnishes a unique exception to this sad trend. Their strategic thrust into the ghetto has been eminently blessed by God. Their youth clubs, adult Bible studies and live-in ministries have fostered revolutionary changes in the lives of numerous Negroes, Mexican-Americans, poor whites and Indians across our nation.

Their emphasis on discipleship is producing solidly based men and women who are being trained to undertake the leadership in the furtherance of the Kingdom of God in urban America. Their cooperation with local urban churches is underscored by the way they are providing training, tools and personnel to assist the indigenous pastor. The key to their success is twofold: a definite call of God to a specific ministry; and a servant-like attitude on the part of their highly dedicated staff.

Everybody's Afraid in the Ghetto documents the miracles the Almighty has performed in placing His imprimatur upon this organization that can best be described as one which incarnates a reckless abandonment of time and energy to God. In one fell swoop Keith Phillips provides a tangible plan and realistic hope for white Americans to experience significant involvement in our great cities. Through the experience of scores of men and women World Impact has put the lie to the belief that an uninvolved spectator-like posture is the only option available to seriously aroused people of God. I commend your reading and contemplation of this positive challenge. I eagerly await your resultant actions.

Edward V. Hill

PREFACE

HOT AUGUST NIGHT

August 11, 1965 was an unusually sultry day in Los Angeles. At 7:00 P.M. California Highway Patrolman Lee Minikus steered his motorcycle along 122nd Street, just south of the Los Angeles City boundary, when a black man alerted him of a drunk driver. Minikus pulled over Marquette Frye, a twenty-one-year-old Negro, at 116th and Avalon, *near* but not *in* Watts. He was driving his mother's 1955 gray-white Buick. At 7:05 Marquette failed a sobriety test. The officer radioed for a squad car and tow truck to impound the vehicle.

Ronald Frye, 22, a passenger in his step-brother's car, was discharged from the United States Air Force a few days before. When Ronald was informed that he could not take Marquette's car home (routine police regulation), which was only two blocks away, Ronald ran for his mother, Rena Frye, aged 49, so she could claim the vehicle. Ronald and his mother returned at 7:15 P.M., the same time Bob Lewis, Minikus' motorcycle partner arrived. Because it was a very warm evening many residents were outside. An original group of thirty swelled to three hundred spectators.

At first, Mrs. Frye scolded Marquette for drinking. Marquette pushed her away. Until then he had been peaceful and cooperative. Now he screamed and swore, "the cops will have to kill me before I go to jail." The patrolman pursued Marquette when he resisted arrest.

Onlookers became hostile. Minikus drew his revolver to hold off the crowd. Three more patrolmen responded to a radio call. Mrs. Frye, now belligerent, jumped on the back of one of the officers and ripped his shirt. Attempting to subdue Marquette, one officer swung at his shoulder with a night stick, missed, and struck him on the forehead. Blood flowed from a minor cut as Ronald struggled with the officers. By 7:23 all three Fryes were under arrest.

It was a steamy night. A restless crowd on the street sought relief from the muggy heat and the boredom of life in a substandard urban area. This period in the history of Watts would well be remembered as a "Hot August Night."

At 7:25 P.M. when the patrol car left with the three prisoners, more than a thousand were in the crowd. One officer was spat on. A young black man and woman were arrested for inciting violence. They spat on a cop. As the last police car left at 7:40 P.M. it was stoned by the now irate mob. Things quieted down—for the moment.

Distorted rumors spread. One rumor held that the Fryes were beaten inside the patrol car. Another rumor declared that the young woman arrested for spitting (who was wearing a barber's smock) was pregnant and had been abused by cops.

4

By 8:15 a reign of terror had begun. The crowd swelled. Restless neighbors had short tempers, induced by the sticky, inescapable heat. Voices grew louder. Soon the original arrest was forgotten, along with the police who had made it.

Officers, cars and buses were the first targets of bricks and rocks, beer, whiskey and wine bottles, concrete blocks and asphalt. Anything light enough to throw and heavy enough to do damage was employed.

Before this tense Wednesday was chronicled into history, marauding bands numbering fifteen hundred had injured nineteen police and damaged fifty vehicles. People yelled, smashed windows, looted and burned with no thought as to why they did it. They couldn't explain their actions if you were to ask them. It was just mob spirit.

Before the Watts riots ceased, fear, death, wanton destruction of property, maiming, aggravated assault, burning, unemployment, heartbreak and pillaging were all employed as adjectives to describe the worst domestic violence since the Civil War. Gun sales went up 250 percent; stores sold their entire stock in hours.

Thursday, August 12, there were 7000 rioters, 350 officers and thousands of terrified residents in Watts. The 10,500-man Fortieth Armored Division of the California National Guard was alerted. A 500-man brigade was on standby orders, according to Major General Charles A. Ott, Jr., Commander.

Armed guards protected firemen from snipers and brick-throwing mobs, whose aim was to prevent fire fighting. An infamous chant vibrated with a deadly echo throughout south central Los Angeles—"Burn, baby, burn." Entire blocks were gutted, blazing automobiles could be seen in every conceivable position. Muzzle

Watts, during the 1965 riots

flashes of guns added to the spectacle. Police guns, National Guard guns, rioters' guns—guns everywhere. Through it all, the unending chant, "Burn, baby, burn." Black non-chanters were suspect: suspicion likely meant a bad beating.

Hundreds of fires—firemen, showered with missiles and bullets, were forced to let fires burn because of insufficient police protection. One fireman was killed and a colleague injured when a wall collapsed on them—a result of arson. Wine bottles became Molotov cocktails. People and cars became the targets for these fire missiles. A bullet hole in a fire engine's windshield was mute evidence of the previous night's horror. Two hundred and one buildings were completely destroyed, 536 extensively devastated with uncounted structures suffering minor damage.

Friday the 13th was the worst day. There were seventy-five injured. Motorists were dragged from their cars and beaten by rioters. The temperature that night never fell below seventy-two degrees. Bruce Moore, a four-year-old Negro boy, was killed by an old boyfriend of his mother's while he sat in his front yard.

Groceries, clothes, guns, ammunition, liquor and television sets were looted. Six-year-old children stole the property of people who were helpless to do anything but watch. What a low form of human activity! Most of the dead in the riots were looters. By midnight one thousand National Guardsmen marched shoulder to shoulder, clearing the street.

On Saturday a curfew was imposed on a twenty-one square mile area from 8:00 P.M. to dawn. By midnight there were 13,900 guardsmen, 934 Los Angeles police and 719 sheriffs.

Sunday night the curfew area was fifty square miles.

Motorists were warned to avoid the Harbor Freeway. Hunger became a problem in south central Los Angeles because markets were destroyed and food rotted in refrigerators without electricity. Medicine was difficult to obtain. Unemployment resulted from burned-out businesses.

When everything was over there were thirty-four dead, 1032 wounded, 3952 arrested (five hundred under eighteen). Two-thirds of the rioters arrested had previous police records. Forty-six million dollars worth of property was destroyed; a horrid epitaph of what society would like to call an illegitimate offspring of unusual times.

Three days before the Watts riot, seven hundred Ku Klux Klan members paraded through Americus, Georgia, protesting against rights claimed by blacks. That same day in Detroit thirty-five hundred Black Muslims screamed "Negro supremacy!" They blamed the white man for all race trouble.

Only five days after President Johnson signed the Voting Rights Act into law, all hell broke loose in Watts. Dr. Harold W. Jones, a Negro psychiatrist who was in Watts during the disturbance, found no guilt in the minds of the rioters. "They feel morally right about what they have done. They look upon it as a revolt rather than a riot and therefore subject to a different value system."

The flames of Watts illumined the stress of the ghetto across America and cast its light on black-white tensions. The volatile social chemicals interacting in urban America had exploded. Watts emerged as an international term synonymous with racial strife. Yet Watts was simply the prelude to a bloody score composed in Newark, South Side Chicago, Harlem and elsewhere.

In 1964 the Urban League rated American cities according to what they offered the average Negro. They placed Los Angeles first among sixty-eight municipalities considered. To state it plainly, Watts had less of a reason to riot than did any other American ghetto.

Yet Watts did riot. Why?

ONE

I walked sadly down 103rd Street, the main thorough-fare in Watts. The smell of battle hung in the air. My mind flashed back to bombed-out streets of Frankfurt, Germany, upon which I had walked as a child with my parents. As the hot August sun beat down upon gutted buildings and blood-spotted cement, I moved among the debris and chaos and mourned for this part of Los Angeles which I had begun to call "my turf," my mission field.

"Hey, Keith, you know what?" It was Billy, a young friend I had led to Christ a few months before.

"My brother, John, he shot this cop!" Billy stood directly in front of me, legs apart, an imaginary gun in his hand. "Bang! Bang, bang!" He pretended to shoot me and then, mimicking the policeman, he clutched his left arm, slumped slowly to the ground, adding, "John said the blood oozed through his fingers and soaked his whole sleeve."

Billy was obviously proud. I was shocked! Then he

10

jumped to his feet, clenched fists pounding the air and boasting, "And my other brother, Hank, he slugged this cop, see. Right in the face. Pow!"

Ralph, Billy's teen-age friend, excitedly chimed in. "I guess we showed 'The Man!' He won't mess with us again without thinkin' twice!"

They rambled for a while. I had to get away and think. I was shaken and disillusioned. This was my first encounter with one of my young friends since the riots and his "wonderful" accounts were like a slap in the face. This alerted me to a new awareness, a very personal awareness, of the hatred and frustration that were brewing in this urban cauldron.

As I stood in the midst of this holocaust, my mind raced with myriads of questions. I questioned God. I questioned my church. I questioned myself. . . .

Was the Prince of Peace ineffective in urban America? This question caused the greatest pain. I knew these people had been forced to see themselves as second-class citizens. *Could the love of Jesus instill a fresh self-image in blacks?* Christ's sacrifice was to save all men and reconcile them to God and to each other. *Would they reject equality before God based on this sacrifice?* I looked around again at this silent street, patrolled by duets of officers, resembling the path of a tornado. *Was violence the only avenue of self-respect left?*

Then my thoughts encompassed my church which had the Good News for the whole world. *But would the white church never accept a brother with a different skin color into their fellowship.*

And what of my own personal ministry? *Could I be a friend here? Could I witness? Or was I born with the wrong skin color?*

As I walked on, taking in painful sights of the cooled-down violence of recent days, I began to sense another, totally new, feeling. Beneath the destruction, the pain, the death, there was a strange carnival-like undercurrent—a distinct new pride in the inhabitants of this well-publicized ghetto. For once in their lives they spoke and the world stood still and listened. What will this infant pride, born of violence, mean to Billy and kids like him who bragged about his brother shooting a cop?

South Central Los Angeles is a hot jungle stuffed with almost half a million people: endless roads, acres of broken glass, gutters flooded with garbage, with rats methodically investigating a stench reminiscent of Hong Kong. Anyone in his right mind would know without a second thought that this is one place he does not want to be. I was beginning to wonder why I was here.

The Outsider

It started in September, 1964, when I entered UCLA at the age of sixteen with dreams of pursuing a career in politics. At that time I became director of Youth for Christ clubs in Los Angeles' inner city and began my routine of driving into the ghetto after completing my morning classes in Westwood.

Urban America was a different world than the distinctively white, middle-class one where I had grown up. If a black man or a brown man walked into my community, he stuck out like a sore thumb. Mothers gathered their children a little closer to them. Businessmen subconsciously rubbed their hands over their rear pockets to reinforce the security of their wallets. Storekeepers protectively intensified their watch over their wares. In a word, "suspicion" flooded the atmosphere.

Now the shoe was on the other foot. I was the one who was different; I was the one who attracted attention and was the object of suspicion. When I arrived at one of the high schools, I walked directly into the building by the closest door and insecurely through the halls enroute to where the YFC club met.

I sensed I was out of place. Everyone stared at me. At least I thought everyone was staring. I knew they were thinking, "He's too young to be a teacher and the wrong color to be a student. Wonder who he is!"

When I entered the room where the Bible club was held, I relaxed because I knew that the guys and gals there cared about me and loved me. After we spent thirty or forty minutes together, I retreated to my trusty 1955 Oldsmobile and charted a direct course for the nearest freeway onramp. I was relieved when my car merged into the "safety" of the slow lane of the freeway.

The first time I drove into Watts I was afraid, skeptical of so many Blacks heavily concentrated in one area. I felt like an outsider in a human prison yard. I caught myself looking down on these creatures who were notorious for prostitution, narcotics, theft and violence.

As the months passed, an astonishing thing happened. The fear turned to compassion. The hate that stemmed from fear started to wane. It wasn't sudden. There was no thunderbolt from heaven. Warm feelings were growing between me and the YFC kids. There was Jim, who insisted on changing my tire after it was punctured by a pin-knife. There was Rosemary, great granddaughter of a slave, who baked a cake for my seventeenth birthday. There were scores of unsolicited smiles, anxious teen-agers wanting to learn of God and live for Christ. There were grateful parents offering help and appreciation.

13

Whether I liked it or not, God was leading me to a mission for which I was completely unprepared, and furthermore, not too turned on about: a mission to the inner city.

The response to this idea was other than warm. One pastor counseled, "Keith, God can use you much more in suburbia and your work here will be rewarding." A peer advised, "You'll waste your talents and your time in the ghetto."

A very unsystematic survey of Christians led me to two discouraging conclusions: (1) Christians conducted a very limited version of what the New Testament outlines as the Christian mission. (2) The mainstream of evangelical Christianity was afraid to get too close to "these people," or of becoming too involved, for fear something might rub off.

This second conclusion was accurately demonstrated by a church with which I was acquainted that sent buses to every surrounding white area to pick up youngsters for Sunday School. But they blatantly bypassed one community, the black and brown housing projects. Perhaps they were afraid that the black and brown children would tear their Sunday School rooms to bits or soil their beautiful pews. When such exclusiveness occurs the church ceases to be the house of God and becomes man's sacred tabernacle. The building becomes holier than the God for whose worship it was built.

God *was* leading me.

As I navigated through the inner city, I saw hundreds of boys and girls who had never heard of the love of God and the exciting news that Jesus died to give them a new life. I failed to see how Christian Americans could spend millions of dollars each year for foreign missions and send hundreds of missionaries abroad while they completely ignored the black, brown, Indian or poor white who totalled 25 percent of our population. The most logical way to win the world was to start with my Jerusalem.

I tried, but I couldn't rationalize away the Los Angeles inner city. I wrestled with the danger factor and questioned whether urban youngsters were really my responsibility. I hadn't read the books that declared a white man could not minister in a black community. Had I done so, I would not be writing this book.

I was well schooled in every man's need for a personal relationship with Christ, and knew that love and happiness came from God alone. I had been taught to share Jesus with others.

But the most visible source of urban anguish was not spiritual; it was the shocking poverty. It was the conspicuous degradation of the masses. How could Christians shut their eyes to avoid seeing hungry children watch their parents drink up the welfare check? Could we damn the poor as merely lazy? Shun the naked? Self-righteously pity the lonely? And what about the brokenhearted?

I determined that to say, "It will be worth it when you get to heaven" is a cop-out. Christ is relevant to their needs NOW. God was leading me to do something about it. My quick trips in and out of the high schools were not enough.

The Projects

In March, 1965, I drove to Jordan Downs Housing Project located in the northeast corner of Watts. What a sight! There were rows and rows of shabby apartments. Rent started at $21.00 per month. Six or seven kids, a mother (seldom a father), in a two-bedroom house was not abnormal. Almost every house could boast a broken win-

15

dow. The roads and cement play areas were laden with glass. Kids ran around barefoot, apparently immune to cut feet. Graffiti on the sides of buildings didn't make any sense to me: "God is the sun" and "Black is not Hell."

Nervous, but expectant, I eased out of my car, checked to make sure the windows were rolled up tightly and all the doors were locked. Five teen-age boys stood by the door of a car about fifteen feet from me. They stopped their conversation and glanced my way—a white dude in their part of town. I wasn't sure what to expect from them. They scared me. I decided to plot my course in the opposite direction. I walked quickly to the first house in sight and boldly knocked on the door. Johnny Davis peeked out through a hole in the door to see who was there. The twelve-year-old asked, "What do you want?"

"My name is Keith, and I was wondering if you'd like to play some football with me. Then I want to tell you and some of your friends a Bible story," was my reply.

"Wait a sec. I'll ask my mom if I can come."

About twenty seconds later a beaming Johnny was at the door. He asked, "Can Tommy come?" Tommy was his ten-year-old brother.

"You bet," I assured him. "Do you have some more friends who'd like to play, too?"

"Sure," said Johnny, "follow me." We went next door and picked up three more boys. Johnny wanted one more friend to come. Joe was to be an important part of our group, because this twelve-year-old boy would be the first to ask Jesus in to control his life.

That first Thursday we had six club members. We went to a recreation field about half a block away. The grass had been trampled into dirt. Debris was everywhere. As we followed the path from "the projects" toward the field, the boys took turns hanging from my arms and legs. Everyone wanted a piggyback ride. Everyone got one. I felt like a long-lost uncle. They weren't surprised that I wanted to play football with them and had no apprehension about being my friends. Each boy was anxious to be touched, listened to and talked with. Each one seemed starved for attention and love. They were noticeably fascinated with the blond hair on my arms. No problems! Instant friends!

I got an education that Thursday. Tommy jerked his head in the direction of the road, "My school is right across the street, right next to the market."

Not to be outdone, Joe told me, "My older brother goes to Jordan High School. He plays basketball there." Jordan High was adjacent to the field on which we sat. A steel mill bordered the high school and the recreation field. A junk yard clung to three sides of the steel mill.

Johnny pointed to the junk yard, "We kill rats in there."

They were anxious to share their mode of life with me and of course I was fascinated.

When there was a slight pause in the conversation, Johnny said, "We can't go out after dark, you know."

"Why?" I asked.

"Cause sometimes guys have fights and shoot guns and things, so Mom makes us stay inside."

"Does your Mom ever take you to the zoo or the circus or the beach?"

"No place like that, Mr. Keith," responded Tommy, "But I go to the store with her once in a while and to the clinic when I'm sick."

It became clear that none of these boys had been farther away than six blocks from this project. As my eyes scanned the community, I saw endless streets of federally-funded apartments choking out any signs of nature—neighbors on

17

both sides and sometimes even upstairs and downstairs. The only other things I saw were the high school, the steel mill and the junk yard. The boundary lines of their world were clearly drawn. I began to feel the isolation of the ghetto.

The kids were more interested in talking than playing football, especially since they had such a captive audience. No doubt my face showed the surprise and shock at some of the things I was learning.

I finally changed the subject, "How would you like to hear a Bible story about one of the biggest men who ever lived?"

"Sure!"

"Great!"

The six boys listened attentively as I acted out both roles of David and Goliath.

Tommy questioned David's weapons, making sure he had heard me right. "Did you say he only had a sling shot and five stones?"

"That's right. God helped David to shoot hard and straight. He didn't need any other weapon. And the best part of this story is that God will help every one of us with our problems if we love and obey Him."

The guys threw each other questioning looks. Maybe they each wanted the other guy to cross examine me. I waited.

Johnny broke the silence, "Will you come back again, Mr. Keith?"

I promised I would.

"Can we bring some other guys?" another voice queried.

"Sure, be here at 3:30 next Thursday after school. I'll see you then."

As I started to walk away, I noticed I had an escort. All

six walked to my car with me. I got in, started the motor, and had to tell them to step back before I could drive away. I waved as I left but from that moment my heart never left the inner city.

Quiet, Boy! Mr. Keith's a Preacher

When I arrived at 3:30 the following Thursday, I didn't have to go to any homes to pick up the kids. They were all waiting for me on the sidewalk beside the recreation field. There was Johnny, bigger than life, pointing to the car as I pulled up. He yelled something that could have been, "There he is, I told you he'd come!"

Joe stood, grinning, with about two dozen boys.

We walked together to the field, divided into two teams and started to play football. Unbelievable! Those kids were great!

Forty-five minutes later the game ended. We walked to the base of a large tree. We met under this tree for the next year. When it rained, we met inside the recreation center. When we got to the tree, we all sat down.

I had a few more things to learn. These 10-, 11- and 12-year-olds had grown up quickly. Jimmie, in an attempt to start conversation with me, asked if I wanted to screw his sister. My face obviously registered shock, because he immediately tried to comfort me, "It's OK, man, she's use' to sleepin' with white men!"

"Quiet, boy! Mr. Keith's a preacher!" yelled Joe. I don't know how it started, but every boy called me "Mr. Keith."

That day I told them a story about Felipe Alou, the great black ball player from the Dominican Republic, who broke into major league baseball with the San Francisco Giants. Felipe accepted Jesus as his Saviour the night before he played his first major league game. He says that

19

knowing Christ is the most important thing in his life.

"Have any of you boys ever asked Jesus to be your Saviour like Felipe did?"

No response.

"Would you like to have Jesus come into your life and be your Friend forever?"

No response. I was let down. Maybe they didn't understand what I was saying. I was sure they weren't all Christians. I wanted at least one of them to discover Jesus.

"OK, fellas, let's close in prayer." They all shut their eyes.

I prayed, "Father, thank You for letting us have a good time today. If there is one boy here who needs to invite You to take control of his life and have his sins forgiven, grant him the courage to talk to me. Thank You, Lord. Amen."

Club was dismissed. Tommy volunteered to check the football into the recreation center. The guys started to disperse.

Then Joe slowly walked toward me, his head slightly lowered, his eyes on the ground. His voice was quiet, "Mr. Keith, I'd like to be a child of God like Felipe Alou, but—well, I've done a whole lot of bad things and I'm not sure God would forgive me if He knew all about them."

I said, "Joe, that's one thing you never have to worry about. God will forgive you."

I put my arm around him and together we knelt down on the hard, mud field, barely shaded by the tree we had gathered under a few moments before.

Joe had tears in his eyes when he prayed, "Jesus, I love You, I'm sorry I've been so bad. I want You to forgive me and take control of my life." A simple but earth-shaking prayer.

20

Then I prayed, and when I opened my eyes I was greeted by a huge smile. Jesus came into Joe's life. "I can feel Him," he said.

We talked about prayer and reading the Bible. I walked to my car and got a *Good News for Modern Man*, which I presented to Joe.

As I drove away that afternoon, I thanked God over and over for the miracle I had just experienced. I was so excited I missed the freeway entrance. God had blessed my beginnings and I felt the affirmation of the Holy Spirit on my work.

Jesus Is Culture Blind

I kept coming back on Thursday afternoons. Each week the club increased numerically. Most of the boys listened well, but it was hard for so many to sit under a tree for fifteen minutes and be quiet. I decided that expansion must be curtailed, so I said no one else could join the club unless someone quit.

Club continued on this way for about a year. Black boys, and some girls too, were hearing about Jesus. The Holy Spirit was doing His thing. I was learning more and more about ghetto life, but my biggest lesson that year was this: *the gospel has the power to meet people where they are, and then to transform their lives—not according to my white, middle-class, western heritage—but according to the will and Word of God.*

A dear old black lady taught me my next lesson.

She and I met occasionally as I walked toward the recreation field or was escorted to my car. She always had a warm, friendly word for me.

"God bless you," she'd say, or "Hello, there, son, I'm praying for you." One day I saw her waiting by my car. She stood straight and determined as if she had a message of great importance for me. And indeed she did.

"Why are you only working here at Jordan Downs?" she asked. "Don't you know there're people all over this area who need to know about Jesus? Where's your faith, boy?"

Her challenge was a real surprise. I was satisfied with the relationships I was establishing with these boys. I came every week into Jordan Downs and shared Jesus, and this woman had the nerve to ask me why I wasn't doing more!

This jarred my thinking. As I drove through Watts, I looked around. Thousands of youngsters were crammed into this infamous square mile, and I worked with less than a hundred. Not so good after all!

That day I prayed that God would give me a vision and a plan for expansion.

Love—The Counterforce

Now I was standing on 103rd Street, the center of Watts, looking at the results of probably the worst racial riot America has ever known. Newspapers and television newscasters were telling the world about Watts. Politicians everywhere were asking for answers.

Black Muslims gained a significant following in Watts as they preached: "If you really want to be free, reject the white man and the white man's God. It was the white man who kept you in slavery for over two centuries, and it was the white man's God that was used as one of the means to secure the bonds."

The riot was a declaration of hate. The violence and insecurity of the ghetto spelled out fear for both residents and visitors. Christ's Gospel of love is the only viable counterforce.

TWO

EVERYBODY'S AFRAID IN THE GHETTO

When I first drove into Watts I was afraid. I continued to be afraid. Something was so drastically different about an entire community being black and me being the only white. Even though I knew the general community was friendly and would protect me, the possibility of being beaten up, stabbed, or jumped was always present. Possibilities increased if a young man was stoned on liquor or drugs, because he could lose control of his senses.

My uniqueness produced insecurity. I constantly asked God for peace. It didn't come all at once. Complete confidence never came. For that matter it never comes to many of the inhabitants.

Oscar Williams, a recreation director, invited me to a Halloween party in Watts. Williams, an All-American and professional football player, stands about 6'8" and weighs 240 pounds. He is as solid as a rock. After he invited me to the party, he said, "By the way, I ain't comin'. No way you're gettin' me into Watts on Halloween without a police escort."

23

If Williams wasn't coming, there was no way he was going to get me into Watts either.

Many residents are scared to death of the young black radicals and don't understand their militancy. Parents are not only afraid to let their children go out, they're afraid to go out themselves after dark, especially on weekends. I wasn't alone in being afraid.

Familiarity lessened fear, exposure destroyed prejudice, and good friends showed me love, often by protecting me.

Mama Jane, a dear black mother of seven children, saved my neck more than once. She was not an especially religious lady, but she was glad I was teaching "religion" to her kids. Three or four times she chased young men away from me as dusk was falling in Watts. She'd get this old broom and start waving it over her head and yelling with all the might her 300 pounds could muster. It was a strange sight, but these young men, who would engage the police in hand-to-hand combat never argued with Mama.

Mama Jane underscores the fact that urban America is a matriarchal society. The mother dominates this world and the people of the community know it and respect her. Fathers are scarce, often coming and going at will. Children are accustomed to a frequent change of men in the home. The only stability they know is their mother.

A Lack of Authority

Parental authority in the home is often lacking. Many relatives, (aunts, grandparents, etc.), are "living in." James, a fourteen-year-old, explains how this happens. His aunt from Georgia, who has four children, came for a visit two years ago—and never left. They live in his apartment today—four brothers, four cousins, a mother, an aunt, a grandfather and James.

When his mother tells James he can't go to the store, he has learned that if he asks another adult there is a good possibility of getting permission. Soon discipline is nonexistent. James believes that if he asks long enough he can get anything he wants. This lack of discipline results in frustration.

A Lack of Money

A familiar ritual in the ghetto is "the hit." Anyone who comes in from the outside is immediately "hit" for money. You may get hit from a 5- or 6-year old—it may be a 25- or 26-year-old. But the odds are that you will get hit. "Got a nickel?" "Can you spare a quarter?" "Hey, how 'bout a buck?"

At first I usually forked over the money. News must have spread like wildfire, because the more I gave the more I was asked. I thought it was gaining me quick friendship. Then I realized friendship and acceptance are two things you cannot buy, and people resent this kind of charity. I further realized that teen-agers were using my money to bolster their supply of liquor and narcotics.

I asked God to direct me in being sensitive to each case. I wanted to help in emergencies if I could, but I also wanted to have the courage not to give money away out of fear.

I soon learned that if a man said he was hungry, he was often thirsty. I never denied a legitimate request that I know of, but often discovered that the hunger was not too great after all, as we entered the diner, where I offered to buy him a meal.

When children "hit" me for money, the word got around that they would have to do some work. The requests decreased significantly as more children heard the reply, "Sweep the gym floor," or "Pick up the paper on the recreation field."

At first I could say "no" to the children easily, but I was afraid to say "no" to the older teen-agers and those in their early twenties, even though I was probably supporting a bad habit. I didn't want to invite trouble over money. One day an 18-year-old boy asked me for a dollar. I told him I wouldn't give it to him. I got into my car and started to drive away. He lifted his foot up to the right rear window and proceeded to smash the chrome around the glass of my 1962 Comet.

I could never predict what reaction I would get when I denied a request for money. Since the Lord did not endow me with untold millions and since I did not like to lie, I discovered the best policy to follow when working in the inner city is not to carry any money at all. Then, when "hit", I could honestly say, "I have no money."

A Lack of Love

Many of the youngsters had never seen a white man in the flesh before. When I got out of my car the young ones would come and hug my leg or cling to my hand. They were thoroughly fascinated with the light brown hair on my arms. They loved to be hugged or swung and would cling to any bit of love I'd offer.

I had to constantly examine my motives. I needed a sincere love for these children as *people* before I could be an effective minister. If I went to Watts with a superior attitude, doing only my missionary duty, or being a social crusader without love, I would be nothing (1 Corinthians 13).

Because our initial contact was as people who loved each other, it was easy to extend a child's love to Christ.

Their reception of Jesus was completely open. They, without question, accepted what the Bible said, believing God also loved them and was deeply interested in their lives.

Help

It was obvious that I needed help to make any significant ripple in this urban lake. I prayed. Where could I go for help?

A friend suggested that Biola College students could teach the Bible, conduct craft and recreation classes, and establish relationships with urban children.

With the possibility of multiplying my ministry through scores of college students I asked the City Park and Recreation Department to provide facilities in which youth clubs could meet. Five areas were made available, four inside Watts and one a mile west of Watts. This done, I shared my vision of many youth clubs in many areas of Watts with the president of Biola College's Student Missionary Union.

Never have I received a more welcome reception. The president said, "We have been praying for something like this. We feel that God wants us to begin something, but we didn't know whom to contact or where to start. It's unbelievable! We prayed for guidance and you walk in."

Anyone who can attribute all the pieces of this puzzle falling into place so easily without the hand of God is more of a mystic than Maharashi Mashiogi.

Two hundred and fifty Biola students responded to the urban challenge, pledging themselves to direct a weekly youth club in Watts. I devised a makeshift training program for the volunteers, organized them into cores, appointed core leaders, and decided which collegians would work with which age group. I alerted them to some of the do's and don'ts that I had learned the hard way.

The night before they made their first Saturday trip to Watts I stayed at Biola. Did I pray! I really didn't know what to expect. Nothing this size, as far as I knew, had ever been tried in a ghetto before. Suppose it started a riot? I left it in God's hands and went to sleep. (God blesses naive faith!)

We got up early Saturday morning and prayed together. At 9:30 A.M. three Biola busses were stuffed with excited but scared volunteers. They didn't know what kind of reaction to expect from the people or what Watts looked like. Many envisioned Watts as a jungle, fenced in by barbed wire with men perched in trees with rifles.

After a final word of prayer in each bus, I watched them as they pulled out of the campus. During the thirty-five-minute drive to Watts there was a lot of speculation as to what to expect. But I knew they would have to see for themselves. When we arrived in Watts the general reaction was one of letdown.

"When do we get to Watts?"

"We're here," I replied.

"Is this all it is?"

"Look at that; gas stations, stores, apartments, just like any other big city!"

"It doesn't look so bad after all!"

The club leaders were dropped off at the five areas. There was no need to announce our presence. Our white skin was as distinctive as a flaring torch in the deep of night. Scads of kids flocked to these white newcomers and shadowed their every move as if following the music of a Pied Piper. Younger children grabbed hold of the collegians' arms and legs, and when our club leaders responded warmly, more youngsters ran to them to be hugged, swung, touched and loved.

The Biola students talked and listened to the children, played games with them, and told them that they would be back next week to talk about Jesus. They got the kids' names and ages and assigned them to clubs.

I was excited! It was the most amazing sight I had ever seen. Hundreds of black children making friends with whites.

Get to Know Them

This started at the end of September, 1967. During the first few months the college students still lived in the shadow of the picture they had of the riots two years before.

Soon real relationships developed. College kids took youngsters on outings, brought them to Biola for basketball games, soccer games, parties, and to spend the night in the dorms.

Of course there were problems. I should have made some kind of glossary of words which the collegians might not understand. I also should have warned them that often the words "God" and "Jesus Christ" were only understood as swear words and associated with things "mean" and "nasty."

(To ask Jesus to "come into my heart" may mean to the child that he would have to swallow Jesus or be cut open and have Jesus put inside.)

Black teen-agers at first were suspicious and stood off to see what was happening. When they saw that we were sincere and faithful, they began asking what we had for them. "You've got these clubs and trips going for our little brothers and sisters, what have you got for us?"

Even today, we start ministering with children to prove ourselves and earn the right to be friends. Then we go on to the teen-agers. Parents are generally happy that we came. We hear these words a hundred times (no exaggeration), "It's good for the kids to be taught religion."

Listening

A major ingredient in the chemistry of any friendship is "listening." One boy came to club with salty white tear stains on his cheeks. His eyes were sad and he was unable to get into the spirit of his games. Randy, the club leader, talked to him and encouraged him to open up.

The child began to cry, "Well, I had this frog, see. I caught him over in the wash, (the Los Angeles River). I made a house for him and I brought him flies and I used to talk to him and he died!" Another torrent of tears.

"He got all stiff and smelly and my mom made me throw him out." More tears. "When I went to school today I told my teacher, Miss Adams, about Charlie (that's his name—Charlie), and Miss Adams laughed!"

Randy put his arm around the boy and they talked for a long time about pets. Randy told about his dog, Buttons, who had been hit by a car. They talked about love and about feeling sad. Randy had taken a real, sincere interest. He had listened, and the friendship was secure.

Understanding

Jackie lived in the Mead housing project a mile from city hall. One afternoon she came to her club leader in tears. Three weeks before, Jackie had accepted Christ as her Saviour. Her club leader gave her a copy of *Good News for Modern Man* and boldly asserted that if Jackie read the Bible she could claim the promises Jesus made in His

Word because she was a child of God now.

Jackie pointed to her Bible on the grass, "It just isn't true," she said, "I don't know what to do because it isn't true!"

The appalled club leader asked what she meant.

"Well, I read something in the Bible and I tried it and it didn't work," was her reply. "It says if we ask anything in Jesus' name it will be given to us."

The college girl went for the normal Christian cop-out, "What did you pray for?" expecting the child had prayed for a selfish thing or something obviously outside the will of God.

Jackie said, "I prayed awfully hard that my mommy and daddy wouldn't get a divorce, but they did anyway. Now Daddy's gone, he doesn't live with us any more."

This was a hard issue to come to terms with. It made each of us stop and see exactly what the Word of God means. Many of the biblical cliches we have known all our lives simply don't apply in every case. A need for deeper understanding forced us to our knees to seek Divine wisdom so we could encourage Jackie and identify with her needs.

Being Faithful

Judy, twelve years old, lived with her mother at the Pecan housing project. Her father, who no longer lived in the home, phoned and arranged to take Judy to Disneyland on Saturday. She was to meet her father at 10:00 A.M.

Saturday, she was on the corner at 9:45. Soon it was 10:30. She waited, but no father. Then it was 11:00. At noon she gave up and walked back into the house. Her daddy didn't show.

He phoned a week later, "I'm sorry about missing the trip to Disneyland, but I'll take you out to dinner after school." He offered no explanation for not showing up last Saturday, but his promise of tomorrow satisfied Judy.

Once again, the next afternoon, the child eagerly waited on the corner. Again, Daddy didn't show.

This kind of thing underscores the urgency of faithfulness. Our college workers promised the children that they would be with them every week. I impressed upon them again and again that if they came for two or three weeks and then, because of a late date Friday or urgent studying, decided to skip going to Watts, the children would lose confidence in them. Their first reaction would be "just like Daddy." The club leader would then have to lay the groundwork again and rebuild confidence in the youngsters that he did care and would be a faithful friend.

Paul states, "It is required in a steward that a man be found faithful" (1 Cor. 4:2). We must be found faithful.

Taking It in Stride

Gail, a college volunteer, stepped off the bus at Nickerson Recreation Center. She was greeted by a ten-year-old boy who proudly held up a dead cat by the tail. Its death had obviously not been recent for behold, "he stinketh." I watched to see what would happen.

Gail, pretty and petite and not much taller than the ten-year-old she faced, never flinched. She took the cat out of the boy's hand, held it firmly by the tail, and deposited it in a garbage can with great dignity. The boy stood with his mouth open. I was shocked, myself. If Gail had screamed, she would no doubt have been met with a dead animal every week.

Gail passed her first test of fire and was one step closer

to being accepted. It is not wise to show surprise or shock at anything. Whatever happens, a good ground rule is "take it in stride and carry on."

One of the fellows nearly blew it when he went home with one of his club members. He entered the apartment and saw filth and dirt which is synonymous with the word "ghetto." He saw four mattresses, side by side, in what was designed to be a living room.

"This is my bedroom," the child explained. He went on and said that ten children and their mother lived in the three-bedroom house.

The club leader's first reaction was that of pity, "Gee, I'm sorry you have to live here." He realized too late, by the look on the kid's face, what he had done. He had stamped out the little pride that still flickered in the child.

It's hard not to over-react when we see extreme poverty and great need. By controlling our emotions we are less likely to offend someone.

Ghetto Is Isolation

After a while, adults in Watts were asking me why I was bringing "detectives" to the housing projects to play with their children. At first I thought they were joking. But it happened too often to be a joke. I asked one of the officers of the Seventy-seventh Precinct why the people thought this was happening.

"It's simple to understand," he said, "the only whites these people ever see in their community are either police officers or merchants. Your volunteers don't have any wares to peddle and they're not uniformed policemen. Therefore, they must be detectives."

"Ghetto," by definition, means isolation. Isolation and ghetto are as intimately related and dependent as stars and constellations. You can't have one without the other.

Many Watts youngsters had never seen a real, live white person face-to-face before. They had seen white people on the TV, in a magazine, or on a billboard, but never in person. Why? Many of them who were twelve years old or younger had never been more than five or six blocks from their home, except when they were born. (There were no hospitals in Watts.) Consequently, the exposure we offered in Watts was remarkable.

An internal ghetto is more devastating than living in a slum. Often the most serious ghetto conditions are inside a person—lack of love, security, acceptance and self-worth.

Jimmy, seven years old, lived in Watts. When I asked him his name he shied away. I figured he was hesitant about talking to a white man. Even after we had spent two hours together he wouldn't tell me his name. It finally occurred to me that he didn't know his name. No one ever bothered to call Jimmy by his name. He was one of ten children called in unison for dinner or for any family gathering. In school and at the playground he was tagged as "you" and "boy."

There is nothing quite so sweet as to be called by your name. That means that the one addressing you believes you are important—so important that he knows and remembers your name. If someone else believes you are important you can feel that way too, and feel it with some degree of security.

"Ghetto" also is a geographic isolation. For instance, one afternoon we loaded a Biola bus with a hundred youngsters for a seven-mile journey to the beach.

When we arrived at the blue Pacific and the kids piled out of the bus, an amazing thing happened. The majority of the kids just stood still and stared at the ocean. They had

34

never seen anything like it. It obviously far surpassed their wildest expectations of how big an ocean could be.

That experience is unforgettable. I had known how big the ocean was ever since I could remember. I was never surprised by its vastness. But, I hadn't grown up in a ghetto. I realize that there are people in middle America who have never seen an ocean, but these kids live only seven miles from one.

Some children we work with have never been in a swimming pool. When we take them swimming they jump in with no hesitancy at all. No, they don't know how to swim, and if misfortune leads them to the deep end, they are soon exploring the bottom, willing or not.

It didn't take long for me to realize that these kids were ignorant of water and its attendant dangers; they had never been exposed to it, they had no fear of it. That thought was sad, but the general principle was encouraging.

Many of these youngsters never realized that they were supposed to hate me because I am white. They had not yet been told that they were not to believe or trust a white person. And, since they were ignorant of this, they were not afraid of me. Indeed, they loved the love I offered them. They were most receptive.

I thank God for the opportunity to work with this very impressionable age while they will still listen to me. They are ready to learn about Jesus and as they grow up, their lives in Christ will mature right along with their physical development. This seemed to be the major area we should concentrate on—the youngster, who simply had not learned it was proper to hate the white.

Don't Know All That Stuff

Conrad, a recreation director, phoned me one afternoon. "Keith, this is Conrad. Get down here on the double and bring a Bible with you." I knew from the tone of his voice he was concerned. Conrad is one of the nicest guys I've ever met. No one ever pushed this 6-foot 4-inch former college football player around. He was firm in his discipline with the kids, but compassionate and kind. I wondered what had happened. He was one of the most highly respected blacks in the community.

When I arrived he handed me a piece of paper with dozens of questions from the Bible. I was puzzled.

"What in the world is this, Conrad?" He looked a little embarrassed, "Those eight boys sit outside my office on the grass there every day reading the Bible. When they come to something they don't understand, they ask me. At first I avoided them, but they became so persistent I answered a couple of questions, but then I discovered there was a lot I didn't kno I wrote their questions down and told them I'd answer them later. Look at this list, Keith, I don't know all that stuff."

I looked at the questions and said, "What did you have in mind, Conrad?"

"How about you giving me the answers and I can tell the boys."

"Great, here's a Bible for you, let's get started."

We got through about three questions when we began a serious discussion on what it means to know Christ. Conrad was open to the influence of the Holy Spirit and it was an easy thing to lead him into the Kingdom.

At the Christmas party that year we had about 800 kids in the gym and Conrad offered the prayer and gave his testimony. When he left the projects to become a coach, we gave him a large family Bible and he was so touched he broke down and cried.

Teaching the Teachers

The youth clubs taught the college volunteers as much as the college students taught the children in Watts. Prayer meetings sprung up spontaneously all over Biola College. Students prayed weekly in groups of seven or eight. At first they prayed for "those kids in Watts" but soon were interceding for individuals.

"Lord, bless David and help him to overcome his hatred for school." "Oh, God, touch Susie's body, it's so hard for her to keep going."

It was a very touching experience for me to attend their prayer meetings. I spent every Wednesday afternoon and evening a Biola. Each time I came away with the feeling that they were as concerned for their friends in Watts as I.

One Biola junior excitedly approached me. The daughter of a pastor, she had been a Christian for twelve years. But that morning she led her first person to Christ. This experience was repeated many times.

Our urban thrust proved to be a practical training ground for the mission field. Students were forced into a cross-cultural experience, demanding that they refine out staunchly imbedded tradition and come to terms with the pure essence of the gospel. You don't have to become "white" to become Christian. (See Acts 15:29.)

Youth clubs provide a great exposure for white, middle-class American collegians. Many are deprived of any contact with blacks. Now they learn that blacks are real people. They have the same drives for security and love we all have. They are not inherently dirty, nasty and stinky. This exposure is worth all the effort.

Don't Be Afraid of Anything

In addition to the college students' exposure, hundreds

of youngsters, teenagers and adults found a *purpose* for living and freedom from fear by surrendering to Christ. But one outstanding biblical principle became incarnate. We fractured a misconception—250 college men and women discovered that white men can and must be used of God in a black ghetto.

Everyone is afraid in the ghetto. People who have lived here for years; people who visit once a year; prostitutes, revolutionaries, gang members, police. Everyone. Physical safety cannot be assured. I memorized the words of Jesus: "And I say to you my friends, do not be afraid of those who kill the body, and after that have no more that they can do. But I will warn you whom to fear: Fear the One who after He has killed has authority to cast into hell; yes, I tell you, fear Him!" (Luke 12:4,5, *NASB*). The psalmist comforts, "Those who love thy law have great peace" (Ps. 119:165, *KJV*). To fearful people, we were bearers of real peace.

THREE

THE TESTS OF FIRE

Once again God was pushing me ahead. I was anxious to use the lessons I had learned in a program that would bring the Kingdom of God to the hearts of the people in Urban America. I wanted to hire fulltime staff, and buy homes so we could live in the inner city. We need to live with those to whom we minister. If I approached a foreign missions board and asked them to sponsor me in a ministry to Haiti, I doubt they would approve of my living in Miami and commuting to Haiti. They would insist I live in Haiti so that I could understand the needs and customs, and feel the pulse of the people. We have to live in the iner city.

Thanks to financial and administrative help from friends, WORLD IMPACT, INC., became an organization in March, 1971. My secretary Carol Froese and I set up busines in a borrowed warehouse—with 10,000 paper clips (Carol explained, "The more you buy, the cheaper they are!"), two borrowed desks, a borrowed typewriter and a telephone. This became the base of our dream to preach Christ across urban America.

Our first task was to put into writing six years of experience with which we could train others. Then we worked out the following strategy for hiring staff.

First, I preached to colleges and churches, always using the Bible as my authority. The Holy Spirit convicts and calls people. I challenge men and women with the crying need of urban America for Christ and our responsibility to minister in our own Jerusalems. I never pull any punches about what the cost is. If anything, I paint the picture gloomier than it is. I want everyone to have a thorough understanding of what is involved. I look for people who are willing to suffer for Christ, and who realize this suffering will not meet with great applause and probably not much tangible sympathy or support, at least at first.

People always ask me if it is safe, especially for girls, to live in the inner city. Can I guarantee their safety? No, of course not. Neither is it safe for white pimps, prostitutes and revolutionaries in the ghetto. They are willing to serve their gods of sex, money and change. Does our God demand less? No, we cannot guarantee safety, but we know that God is in control.

Then I check for a few specific characteristics in potential staff. Primary is a real love of God. Young people find it easier to adapt to a new culture, have less ties to keep them from a reckless abandonment to God, and are usually more accepting of a different color-culture.

Everyone is asked to participate in youth clubs, Bible studies or teen-age activities. As they minister I observe them. Once they prove their sincere call and "servant-hood," we talk about full-time status.

Keith Phillips, founder of World Impact, Inc.

Next is the process of New Testament discipleship—building our staff. I invest in each one everything I have learned and try to give intimate personal guidance without stifling personalities and talents. I work closely with each one, measuring how much he can do on his own and then allow him to step out.

The P.T.L. House

I needed a house in central Los Angeles. A friend suggested a place a block and a half from the University of Southern California campus. The first time I walked into this dark two-story structure, a fourteen-year-old boy asked me how long I was going to stay.

I knew what the boy was implying, so I replied, "You don't understand. I'm a minister."

"That's okay, you don't have to worry," he said, "I won't tell."

It took me five minutes to convince this boy, who was pimping for his mother, that I was only interested in a tour of his home. As I walked through the main floor the musty smell and falling plaster suggested faulty plumbing. The three bedrooms and kitchen upstairs were crowded with people so I surveyed it from a central hall. In spite of the dirt and run-down condition, I felt that 711 West Thirty-second Street had a lot of potential. It's in the heart of a Mexican and black community. Scores of gangs claim the land within one square mile to be their "turf."

When I walked outside into the black night, I saw by moonlight the white-painted Mexican slogans plastered all over the building. This sight sent a weird sensation through me. What an opportunity for ministry! I wanted to shout, but I said it softly, "Praise the Lord!"

Those three words became so associated with my per-

P.T.L. House

sonal feelings about the house that we named it the "PTL" house. We boarded up windows and doors to discourage unfriendly "dudes" from coming and going at will. We wanted to avoid any further pilfering and destruction. Then some of the staff men moved in.

Mark

One afternoon I was sitting at my desk in my office. For some unusual reason, I answered the phone when it rang. Carol usually does.

"I'd like to speak to Rev. Keith Phillips," said a young man's voice on the other end of the line. When I told him who I was, there was a long silence.

43

"Are you still there?" I asked.

"Yea, I'm here. My name is Mark Pendl. I'd like to have an appointment to talk with you some time if I could."

"Well, I'll be leaving town soon. Is it urgent?"

"I think it's pretty urgent. You see, I've been sitting here praying about God's will for my life. I told Him that if He wanted me to work in Watts to have you personally answer the phone. When you answered, I nearly fell off my chair."

Now my end of the line was silent. We had been praying for another man to minister at the PTL house.

"Where did you hear about me, Mark?"

"Well, about three months ago I attended a conference when I was passing through Colorado. Dr. Hill preached and God really touched me. You know Dr. Hill, of course."

Dr. Edward Hill is pastor of Mt. Zion Baptist Church in Los Angeles and is a board member of World Impact. "Yes," I said, "I know him."

"He suggested I call you if I ever got to Los Angeles and I have some relatives here, so I came. I prayed a lot about it and decided to put out this fleece of your answering the phone."

Two things stood out about Mark when I met him: his love for God and his sincerity about his call to the ministry. I told him to get in contact with the fellows at the PTL house and stay with them while I was out of town. I've seen many who feel called to the inner city, but can't endure living there.

Mark had an immediate rapport with the community. I was sure he'd be with us for a long time and I was willing to spend time with him and disciple him.

At first, Mark was impetuous. He wanted to start right

Mark Pendl (right) and friend

out holding street meetings. Through experience we have learned that you cannot move into the inner city on Monday and start preaching on Tuesday. You have to earn a right to be heard by the way you live. Teen-agers and adults watch how you relate to children in youth clubs and determine if you can be trusted. Consequently, I put my foot down and insisted Mark work only with children in youth clubs at the beginning. Working with children was hard for Mark. It tried his patience. But he submitted and did very well. The kids really took to him.

The more I prayed for and with Mark, the more I knew God had a wonderful work for him. As we walked the streets, during that first year, I was amazed at the way the community knew and respected him. Nobody is under any illusion as to why he's there. He's a minister and they know it. He loves God and wants them to love God. People yell, "Hey, Mark what's happenin'," from passing cars. Kids run out and say, "Hi, Marcos."

Superman

Mark knew that the kids in his club were sniffing paint. They'd put spray paint on an old piece of cloth and sniff during club meetings when Mark turned his head. He asked Jackson, an eight-year-old, why he sniffed paint.

"Cheapest way I know to get high," he said, "I like to get high and then play cowboys. Man, I feel just like Superman and I can lick anyone. I also see all kinds of armies and horses and everything when I'm playing."

It's sad that these children resort to sniffing paint to stimulate their imaginations so that they can forget their loneliness, neglect and insecurity.

We learned later that Jackson almost died from sniffing. He inhaled so much paint that he started coughing up

46

paint clots that had formed in his lungs. He broke his paint sniffing habit by turning to harder drugs. Today he's an addict.

The Indian

Mark became good friends with a Navaho Indian neighbor, Johnny White. The first day Mark moved into the PTL house, Johnny greeted him in the front yard and asked, "What are you doing here?"

"I came to share Christ," was Mark's honest reply.

"Is that right? Listen, if Jesus could ever stop me from drinking, then He is who He claimed to be, the Son of God."

"Of course He can stop you from drinking. He's done greater miracles than that."

"Huh, that would be the biggest miracle in the whole world," Johnny shook his head and walked away. One night Mark woke up from a sound sleep sensing that someone was in his room. He saw two shadows at the foot of his bed, a big one and a little one.

It was Johnny and his six-year-old son.

"Mark, Mark, wake up," Johnny was saying, "Mark, come on over and play chess with me, I feel like drinking." There were many nights and many chess games. Sometimes they'd play and talk most of the night.

Johnny had a wife and six children and he was concerned about them when he was sober. The night that Mark laid the gospel on Johnny pretty heavily, Johnny said, with tears in his eyes, "Mark, by the end of 1973 I would like to see my family become Christians."

Johnny had been brought up in a mission on a Navaho Reservation in Arizona, and had accepted Christ as a small child.

47

"Johnny," Mark would often say, "You've got to stop your drinking. You've got to try harder."

"I'm trying, Mark, but then I get this terrible feeling of being all alone and the only thing that helps is getting drunk."

"Just call me whenever you feel that way and I'll come over and talk and we'll play chess."

"Okay, Mark, I'll call you." But Mark was forever finding him drunk. Sometimes he'd be drunk for days. During these times Mark found it impossible to talk with him. One day Mark became frustrated and said, "Johnny, if you don't leave that bottle alone, it will kill you."

And it did just that. Johnny was in the hospital one week before he died. He and Mark had become very close, but Mark felt powerless to help his friend in his greatest need. However, before 1973 was over, Mark saw three of Johnny's children find Christ.

Lucifer

The first time Mark met Robert, a young black man, they were both in the apartment of Elmer, a USC student. Mark was talking to Elmer when Robert interrupted with a statement addressed to Mark, "I know who you are and I know what you're doing." His eyes shot a penetrating stare at Mark.

All during that evening, Mark felt that Robert was constantly aware of him. When Mark started home, Robert said he'd walk with him. As they cut through a dark alley on their way to the PTL house, Robert said, "Mark, I'm controlled by the devil."

Nothing more was said until they reached the front of the PTL house. Robert stood "nose to nose" to Mark without speaking for several moments. Then he put the palms of his hands together, as if in prayer, bowed his head and said, "As we get to know one another better, I hope no harm comes to either of us."

The next time Mark saw Robert it was a warm evening about ten o'clock. Mark started outside to do his nightly jogging, and there stood Robert with two other men. They said they wanted to talk about Christ.

As they talked, Mark felt a strong demonic power in the room. After about a half hour he asked if the two other fellows would leave so he and Robert could talk freely. Robert agreed and the guys left.

As Mark talked with Robert about the love of Jesus and what He could do personally for him, Robert took on an entirely new appearance. His face became distorted and a strange satanic voice spoke from his mouth, "Why are you tampering with my son?" Mark's first reaction was not fear but anger.

"I command you, demon, in the name of Jesus to be quiet." Mark prayed, with his eyes glued on Robert. The demon gave a haunting laugh that increased Mark's courage.

The demon said there is a heaven, a hell and a Jesus Christ. He said that the 144,000 which will reign in the new kingdom will be demons.

Mark said, "That's a lie! You obviously know the Bible, but you are full of lies! You better shut up." The demon mumbled on. Mark, furious at the repeated lies screamed, "I said, Shut up!" The demon quieted down. (Two other staff men, Thuan and Dan, joined in prayer for Robert.) Mark and Robert talked until 12:30 A.M. Robert wanted to ask Christ into his life, but Mark knew the demon (or demons) had to be cast out before Christ could come in.

Mark felt he didn't have the power, so he called me on the phone.

Twenty minutes later I arrived at the PTL house and met Robert. He sat in a trance-like position, lonely and dejected. Under a long black wig I saw eyes that were piercing and hateful. Yet he trembled with fear.

I spoke to the demons, asking their names. One said his name was Ud, the other Death. They spoke with two different voices.

Suddenly Robert assumed a relatively normal composure again. I asked him some questions, "Robert, would you like to become a Christian and be freed from the bondage of Satan?"

"I want it more than anything," he cried, "I am a child of the devil and it's a lonely life."

He described the hatred he felt and the deprivation.

"Do you know who Jesus Christ is?" I asked.

"Yes."

"Do you believe that He is the Son of God?"

"Yes."

"Do you believe that Christ can overcome Satan and take away your sins and give you a new freedom in Him?"

Again he answered that he did.

I told him that I was going to pray in the name of Jesus that "Ud" and "Death" would be cast out of him.

He said, "That would be good."

Dan, Thuan and Mark were all on their knees. I began, "In the name of Jesus Christ. . . ."

But I never got the words "Ud and Death, I command you to flee from Robert" out. My words were interrupted by violent screams and the insane behavior of Robert as he jumped up and down on the couch.

It took about a half hour for Robert to calm down

again. When he regained his composure, I asked him if he had a shrine where he worshiped the devil.

He said he did.

"Do you have the sixth and seventh books of Moses?"

"Yes, I do."

"Robert, are you willing to destroy those and completely end your connection and loyalty to Lucifer? Are you willing to die to him and thereby become alive to God?"

"I can't do it. 'They' wouldn't let me touch those things to destroy them," he said, "They'd kill me before I could reach my relics or shrine."

"They won't hurt me," I said confidently, "I'm protected by the blood of Jesus Christ. Give me the key to your apartment. Let me go get them. I'll destroy them."

"I can't allow you to do that," Robert screamed, "if I do, hundreds will die."

Robert left the house and the four of us sat and talked for a long time. We felt the power of God with us, but we were convicted that we had not been able to help Robert. We prayed that the Holy Spirit would control every part of our bodies. We felt that we had not given ourselves to God as thoroughly as Robert had given himself to Satan. Satan was able to speak through Robert's lips.

In Robert we see a massive trend in America today: people want to experience all the blessings, freedom and peace Christ offers, but they are not willing to give up their allegiance to Satan.

In less than one year God gave Mark rich, practical experiences. Mark's compassion was deepened by the sad helpless feeling of watching eight-year-old Jackson escalate from glue-sniffing to hard narcotics. The death of Johnny, the alcoholic Indian, illustrated the loneliness that leads to futile escapism. Then Robert's refusal to

51

denounce his satanic ties in return for the peace of God characterized the lostness of the inner city.

Narcotics. alcoholism. satanism. Why would God confront Mark in such an *intimate* way with these sicknesses of society? What was God doing? What lessons were to be learned? These were "tests of fire" to prepare Mark for a brand new ministry where alcoholism, narcotics and satanism are a way of life. Mark needed to learn compassion; he needed a faith in God that would bring peace in the face of defeat; he needed to know that Christ is performing miracles. He needed patience to wait for God's timing. Mark's life-long work would demand these characteristics.

FOUR

GATEWAY TO THE GANGS

The night in Colorado that Mark responded to God's call to preach, he thought of his ministry in terms of the David Wilkerson books he had read. He wanted to work with gangs, but had the misconception that gangs didn't exist any more. He thought the inner city would be full of "hippie-type" kids, standing around on street corners stoned on drugs.

He wasn't in Los Angeles long until he realized there were indeed gangs in his neighborhood. There was a gang fight right in the front yard of the PTL house.

One night the Scorpions got high on drugs and thought they could conquer the world. They plowed into a rival gang with ball bats, lead pipes, guns and switchblades. The next morning a seventeen-year-old member of the Scorpions was found stabbed to death in front of the Metropolitan Community Church, a homosexual church.

As Mark read the newspaper account, he felt a strong tug on his heart. He remembered the night he was called to preach. "God," he prayed, "this killing was so useless. Use me, Lord. Help me to lead gang members to Christ."

That very day Mark started to walk the streets of central Los Angeles, hoping to meet gang members. His first contact came with the "little people." These seven- and eight-year-olds are the junior affiliates of the big gangs. They steal, vandalize and cause general havoc. But their notoriety is this: twenty or twenty-five "little people" jump on some unsuspecting person, swarm all over him, cling to him like a bunch of leeches, forcing him to the ground. They often thrust pin knives into the victim's flesh, beat him severely and rob him. Then they flee in every direction. (The members of one such gang in Watts call themselves "The Birds" after the Alfred Hitchcock movie.)

Through the "little people" Mark met Diego Reyes, the leader of the Scorpions, an 800-member Chicano gang. Diego's background resembled that of most ghetto youth with one glaring difference: his mother had taught him about the love of Christ. Diego accepted Jesus as his personal Saviour when he was a child. As he grew older, he had a tremendous desire to belong to something. There was no church, so, he started his own gang.

Diego confided in Mark, "I am sick inside about the way I am living."

Mark told him frankly that Jesus wanted to be the Lord of his life. Diego's relationship with Christ grew along with his friendship with Mark. It helped Mark to have Diego as a friend. He introduced Mark to the president and vice president of many gangs. One afternoon, Diego and Mark were sitting on the front steps of the PTL house, talking.

54

Mark Pendl on steps of P.T.L. House

Diego said, "Marcos, you are my true friend. My house is your house. Don't even knock, just walk in."

Diego's house is the "party house" for the gang. Weekends, up to one-hundred kids gather to drink, gamble, shoot up, sniff, screw, and plan rumbles. Mark talks freely about God with these gang members.

One night, the smell of weed was so intense that Mark stepped outside for a breath of fresh air. A heavyset, black girl and a slight Mexican girl were fighting over which one was the best prostitute for their gang members. The argument soon spread to an all-out girls fight.

These girls are normally reserved for sex, parties or to attend to wounds. But, this night they started an all-out rumble. The black girl was kidnapped into a car by the Chicano girls' gang and thrown out of the vehicle as it was cruising down the street. The boy counterparts of the gang, following close behind in another car, ran over her.

In the midst of all this excitement, one of the boys threw up his hands and exclaimed to Mark, "Man, this is great! This is what we live for!"

The Funeral

Juan was sixteen. He tried to kill Mark one night at a gang party at Diego's house. He sneaked up behind him, cocked his arm over his head, and started to thrust a screwdriver in Mark's back. He would have succeeded had other members of the gang not stopped him. Mark felt such a compassion for these street kids that the attempted murder only increased his love. He and Juan developed a close friendship over the next few months. They talked for hours about Jesus. Juan and many of his friends were very close to accepting Christ when Mark went home to Indiana for Christmas.

Mark wanted to move into an apartment in the Scorpions turf. We prayed about it. I felt that Mark was ready. He had matured from wanting to stand on the street corner and preach to masses, to having a compassion for individuals. Now, he was a genuine friend. He had become a part of the city. I trusted him and never doubted that he had become a man of God.

Mark moved into an apartment on Twenty-fourth Street, the center of gang violence and activity in central Los Angeles. Six hours later Juan was shot in the back of the head with a .38 revolver by four drunken transients from Tijuana. He died in the yard next door. Mark cried in grief, disappointment and discouragement. It was too late! Juan's father asked Mark to speak at the funeral on behalf of the family and the gang members. The Catholic priest instructed the 250 people in attendance to light candles, say rosaries, pray and give to the church in hopes of shortening Juan's stay in purgatory. Then Mark spoke on 1 John, chapter 2, which explains how you can know whether or not you are a Christian. He concluded his remarks with, "How many more of your coffins will I stand over before you come to Christ?" (Since that time he has buried many of those he spoke to.)

Many of the 200 gang members at the funeral spoke to Mark after the service and told him they wanted to hear more about God. Mark began Bible studies with them in his apartment. He soon learned that many of them needed help in reading because they dropped out of school before the third grade. They fear the open school ground will make them easy targets for rival gangs' sniper bullets or knives. This began what Mark calls his "evangelism through literacy" program. He teaches English grammar to the gang members regularly.

I'll Hang Their Bodies

Mark's apartment is right across the street from the Reyes family. He is almost a member of the family. He calls Mrs. Reyes "Mom" and she loves him like a son, prays for him and supports him fully in his ministry. Her four sons, Diego, Pedro, David and Miguel were all gang members.

One weekend, Mark was away visiting friends. When he returned Monday morning, David, the Reyes' youngest son, ran to Mark and said, "Marcos, my mom wants to see you right away about the funeral."

Mark was completely puzzled. David kept talking about a death. He looked at him and said, "Who died?" David just kept rambling on about the funeral and the death.

Mark asked again, "Who died?"

Finally David seemed to hear him for the first time, "Marcos, you mean you don't even know who died? My brother, Pedro, is dead."

Mark's heart hit the bottom of his stomach as he ran across the street to the house. When he opened the door, there sat Mrs. Reyes, dressed in black, a piece of black lace over her head. She was crying. When she saw Mark, she sobbed, "Pedro is dead. Pedro is dead."

Mark felt the sorrow and the hurt because Pedro was a friend, but also because of his love for Mrs. Reyes. She had always been so full of joy and happiness. He had never seen her in tears. He knelt beside her and she said softly, "Pray for me, Marcos, pray for us all." As Mark held her hand and began to pray out loud, he felt a surge of spiritual strength flow between them.

When he finished, she said, "Marcos, I want you to

make all the arrangements for the funeral and I want you to preach."

"Okay, Mom, sure, I'll be glad to."

Still uncertain of any of the details, he took Rosa, a younger sister, aside and asked, "How did it happen, Rosa, how did Pedro die?"

"He was killed in an argument over some car rims. I don't know all the details either."

David took Mark into the back room and showed him a big picture of Pedro, and said, "Look, this is my brother, Pedro, he's dead now, he's dead. He was my best friend. The last words he said were, 'David, David.' He gave me everything, his car—everything. He's dead now."

Just then Diego entered the room. Mark expressed his sorrow. They went out and sat on the front steps. Diego put his head in his hands and didn't say anything for a long time.

Mark could hear "Mom" crying inside and soon the whole thing was too much to bear. Hot tears welled up in his eyes and a big sob gushed from his throat. Diego spoke sharply, "Don't you cry. You have to keep cool because if you break, we all break."

Mark got up and walked home, overwhelmed with the responsibility that was his.

Later that day he and Diego took Pedro's clothes to the funeral home, made the arrangements, and picked out a casket. Mark set the time for the service and the calling hours.

He had never held an entire funeral service before. A lot of prayer and preparation went into his sermon. He knew he must speak words of comfort to the family, but he also knew the gang would be there and he must make the claims of Christ clear.

The day of the funeral he stood near the casket and watched the gang members come down the aisle to view Pedro's body. There were proud kids who sauntered up in their black trench coats and pointed black leather boots. Other kids in khakis, T-shirts and bandanas just stood and stared. The prostitutes, with their bright clothes and dark makeup, sobbed.

Some came to the casket solemnly, genuflected and made the sign of the cross. Others came with tears rolling down their cheeks, hard kids who had switchblades or razor blades in their pockets or purses even then. Mark preached to them all.

Mark will always be haunted by the memory of Mr. Reyes as he stood and stared at his son's body through the entire sermon. Then when it was over, he tearfully lifted Pedro in his arms and hugged him.

The emptiness. He watched Diego standing by, crying, as they put the coffin on the rollers and slid it into the hearse.

After the funeral, Miguel, another brother expressed his hatred. "Mark, if I ever find those guys who killed Pedro, I'll shoot them as many times as I can, then I'll stab them as many times as I can, then I'll cut off their arms and legs and throw them in the street. Then I'll hang their bodies up for public display. After that I'll cut off their heads and put them in a brown paper bag and give them to my mother."

It is difficult for us to understand such hatred. Life in the ghetto is charred with violence. Gang members are unable to channel hostility and frustration into rational courses of action.

I'll Die in My Barrio

The reason there are still thousands of these gangs,

is directly linked to broken homes and poor domestic environment of which these gang members are products. The gang replaces the home. Chino, a fourteen-year-old gang member, was busted for possession of thirteen grams of hash. While at juvenile hall he confided, "My mother doesn't want me around. No one loves me."

Protection is the second incentive. A geographical area where one gang rules is a "turf." To violate someone else's turf is an act worthy of death. A member of another gang doesn't walk across your turf for any reason . . . to go to school or even to the market, without the real possibility of being attacked. Cisco was arrested for assault and attempted murder. He shot a Mexican boy in an intra-barrio dispute over geographical boundaries. Gang members feel secure on their own turf. They fight and even kill to protect the integrity of the turf.

The excitement of violence is another major cause for gangs. Rumbles start because of a thirst for revenge or because one gang, stoned out of their minds, wants to incarnate their supernatural feelings and prove their greatness. The inability to channel hostility into rational courses of action leads to rumbles. This inability results from insecurity. When Mario accused Juan's girl friend of being a "cheap slut" Juan's immediate reaction was to pull a switchblade and stab Mario six times in the shoulder and arm. "What else could I do?" he demanded.

In a two-week period there were five gang related murders near Mark's apartment. One victim was stabbed at 5:00 P.M.—in broad daylight. There was a robbery slaying at a gas station; the victim was stabbed fifteen times. Poncho talked about the brutality of this slaying, "When you stick a guy and he screams, it makes you even more scared, so you just keep doing it 'till he's still."

61

Mark and Chino

Drugs, prostitution, broken homes, alcohol, fear, school violence, poverty, racial hatred and prejudice are by-products of urban gangs. The average gang member, away from the crowd, is a pretty good guy. He's mild, shy and insecure. He wants to know the meaning to life. He needs to hear the gospel of Christ. But more important he needs to see Christ lived. We must take Christ to the gangs.

A slogan plastered on a 24th street building tells their despair: "I was born in the barrio, I live in the barrio, I'll die in my barrio."

FIVE

THE HOUSE WITH GREAT POTENTIAL

Mary Thiessen seemed to be "one of the boys," constantly throwing one line jabs and puns at anyone who left himself open. She was highly intelligent, but I wondered if she were ever serious.

I met Mary during an Urban Encounter in Los Angeles. An Urban Encounter is a three-week orientation to the inner city. College young people live in the inner city, spend time at places like Teen Challenge, a Jesus People Commune or the city rescue mission. We give them a brief, but accurate feeling of the city.

Soon, I saw a different Mary. The glibness wore off and I began to know a determined and serious young lady who was struggling with demands God was putting on her. Mary and I talked for a long time one day about God's standard as outlined in the New Testament and how most people water it down. She showed a lot of insight.

"I see Christians falling into two categories," she said, "those who seem very spiritual but are useless and impractical, and those who are aware of what's happening in the world but reject the power of the Spirit of God."

I was curious. "Where would you put yourself, Mary?"

"I'm not sure," she mused, "I guess I'm so sick of the shallow faith of each group that I don't want any part of either of them." Mary's green eyes, usually radiating sunshine and humor, were soft and solemn as she added, "I can't put it all into words yet, Keith, but I'm seeing some very exciting things here in the lives of the staff of World Impact. I want so much to experience the *power* of Christianity and maybe, just maybe, I'm seeing it here."

"This doesn't sound like the same girl talking who was accused of being on an 'intellectual trip' by one of the fellows the other day," I said, "Didn't you say intellectual pursuits helped you to find God?"

She laughed, "Well, to be frank, I've enjoyed these three years at Tabor College—studying, expanding my mind. Being in a scholastic atmosphere is fulfilling and I'm seriously thinking of a career that will keep me studying and growing. Maybe I'll go on to graduate school and become a professor in a Christian college. I'd like that."

I discovered later that Mary had not wanted to come to the Urban Encounter. One of her professors suggested that she apply. She had stalled until she was sure it would be too late.

"I'd be willing to go, but I'm sure it's too late," she told the professor, "they're probably all filled up."

He immediately called to see if there was room for one more. There was.

Mary agreed to go, feeling that God, through the professor, was pushing her into this. She had no desire to

Mary Thiessen

see Los Angeles nor work in an inner-city situation. Furthermore, and probably the greater reason, she had a gnawing fear that once she became aware of an urgent need, God would hold her responsible to do something about it.

Here in Los Angeles, God was speaking to Mary. She was fighting the whole notion that He would ever call her to such a work. She and her friend, Carol Zerbe, spent many hours together discussing and praying about God's will. Many evenings Mary tearfully tried to rationalize the feelings she was having.

When Mary came for the Urban Encounter in January, 1972, there was no inner-city facility for women staff members to live in. She and Carol lived with a black Christian lady during the Encounter. As the girls were taken to various places in the city, Mary became more impressed with the World Impact staff and their abilities to put their faith to practical tasks.

The night the group went to Bridge Back, a narcotics rehabilitation center, she didn't want to go, but couldn't stand to be alone either. She didn't hear a word of the lecture; her mind was busy analyzing her own problem.

Suddenly she prayed, "God, if You want me, it's OK." That was all. God's Spirit immediately touched her with a pervading joy that overflowed and became so obvious that friends noticed the change.

"What happened to you during the lecture?" someone asked.

"I'll go anywhere for God," was her reply, "I could even start a girls' home in L.A." She took a bunch of girls out to celebrate what she calls her super spiritual experience.

Two weeks later, back in Kansas, I asked Mary and Carol to come to Los Angeles for the summer to start a girls' home. I was unaware of Mary's experience with God in Los Angeles.

Mary hesitated for a moment and then said, "Keith, I'm so shocked that you asked me to do this."

"Why?"

"Because when I was in Los Angeles I felt God might be calling me to do just that," she paused. "I don't know what to say."

"Mary, when you ask God to hit you over the head about something and He does it, do you say, 'Hit me again, God, so I know it was You'?"

Mary agreed to come.

You'll Be Sorry

On the completion of Tabor's 1972 school year, Mary met Carol Zerbe in Montana. They drove straight to Los Angeles, stopping only for four hours on the side of the road to sleep.

Neither had driven the Los Angeles freeway system before. They were going forty miles per hour in the fast lane when a squad car pulled alongside. The officer called over the loudspeaker and instructed them to get into the slow lane. The girls attempted to comply with the outspoken policeman. After missing a few freeway exits, they arrived at our Los Angeles office.

All summer long we expected God to drop a girls' house into our laps. We prayed. Nothing happened. God had other plans for Mary and Carol. They first lived with a suburban family in the San Fernando Valley, then with a black pastor and his family in the inner city, and finally with a seventy-two-year-old black lady in Watts.

We began our summer ministry that year by canvassing a housing project in Watts. The first words we heard from anyone living at the project were uttered by a small boy, "You better get out of here or you'll be sorry."

As our staff handed out fliers announcing a Bible School program which would begin the next day, a handful of boys and girls from the project followed along behind, often taunting and mocking us. Since the small boy's ominous prediction, an atmosphere of gloom seemed to prevail. One woman scolded us for walking on her grass.

A group of black teen-agers lurked in store fronts and doorways across the street waiting for us to make a wrong move. Becky, a fourteen-year-old black girl, well-known as an instigator of trouble at the project, suddenly appeared from nowhere and tried to hit Mary.

Mary grabbed Becky's wrists, held them and laughed, "Hey, you better watch out who you pick on, I have six brothers and I know how to defend myself." Becky turned on one of the other girls, Jeanette, and said, "I'm gonna hit you!"

This had happened to Jeanette once before and she had confronted her young adversary with a positive turn-the-other-cheek attitude and he had walked away embarrassed. It didn't work with Becky. Jeanette stood there calmly and the girl hit her in the back. Jeanette turned pale. No one knew what to do. They felt completely surrounded by hostility.

Becky was aware that Carol would be a challenge also, so she linked arms with Carol and Mary and yelled to the fellows across the street, "Here are two girls for sale! These girls are available!" Mary was really frightened.

Carol, a missionary kid, had experienced many situations where God had protected her. She honestly wasn't afraid. Mary *was* afraid. She wondered if she could face her class tomorrow at the project. That night Mary and Carol had a long talk about fear.

Once again the girls prayed and God answered and gave Mary a peace and calm that continues to this day. From that experience, Mary says, "God showed me that a Christian in the will of God is safer in the most dangerous place than a Christian out of the will of God in the safest place."

During their talk that night, Carol told Mary not to be protective of her. She said, "Mary, please don't interfere if you think you see me in trouble with these kids. God will take care of me."

Next day scores of children came to Bible School and many accepted Christ. Becky dropped by each day for a short time. She really seemed to like Carol. On the third day when Carol asked her to please talk quietly and not disturb the others, Becky clenched her fists and pelted Carol with blow after blow. Mary stood by and prayed, "Lord, protect her, help her!"

Tears crept into Carol's eyes.

Furiously Becky demanded, "Why are you crying?"

Carol answered, "I love you, Becky, and I feel badly because you are angry with me."

This seemed to make Becky more exasperated and she screamed, "Why don't you hit me back?"

Carol said, "I don't want to hit you, Becky, that isn't the answer. I love you and I don't want to hurt you."

Mary felt that by this time she had kept her promise to Carol and she said, "Becky, why don't you get in the car and I'll drive you home."

Becky mocked her words sarcastically, "You'll drive *me* home!"

"Sure I will, come on," Mary walked toward the door

and Becky followed. Carol went too. When they got to Becky's house, the family was too drunk for introductions.

Becky came to club all that summer but never got totally involved. She would always sit back and watch. Once Becky went with the group to the beach. She and Mary were lying in the sun watching the children play. Becky said, "Mary, do you love me?" Mary felt it would be meaningless to answer because she had told her many times that she loved her. So she answered with a question, "What do you think?"

"I don't know, lots of people in the projects are saying that you whites just come down here because some church pays you. They say you really hate us but are doing this to gain status with God."

"What do you think, Becky?"

Becky was quiet for a long time and finally answered, "Yes, I think you really do love me, Mary, but it's hard for me to answer the other people."

Letters to God

Mary came to realize that summer that the teen-age girls in her club had a difficult time expressing their feelings about God in front of one another. Mary suggested they write letters to God. Here are some of them:

"Dear God, I do believe in you no matter what people say, like they be writing on walls and churches, they be writing 'God is the sun,' but I know you are not the sun. You is my father. I do believe that you sent your son down here to die for us. I have faith in you, Lord. Lord, I try to be good but the devil keep coming in the way. Help me, Lord, because you love me and I love you. So help me.

Naomi"

"I want to learn about God. I love God very much and he love me and we are to obey our mother and father.

Diane"

"Dear God, I know that every thing is possible with you. And I choose you to come in to my life from here on.

Janet"

"I want to learn about God. He love everyone in the world. He have power. He die for our sins.

Becky"

The last day of club, Mary asked them what they wanted to talk about.

Becky said, "Tell us how to become Christians again." When Mary explained the way of salvation again, Becky begged her, "Please walk me home, Mary."

When they got to Becky's house, Mary said, "You really want to accept Jesus, don't you?"

"Yes, but . . ." then pointing to the housing project, she said, "it wouldn't be possible here." Then she turned and walked into the house.

Mary walked to the recreation center brushing away the tears. Later Becky told her, "I threw myself down on the bed, and cried, and cried, and cried. . . ."

A Mansion in Disguise

One week before Mary was to return for her final semester of college, I sent her and Carol house hunting. The girls learned a lot about the area driving up and down the streets on hot, muggy days. When we found a house, Carol Froese shared the need for money with her home church in San Jose. They took a love offering which

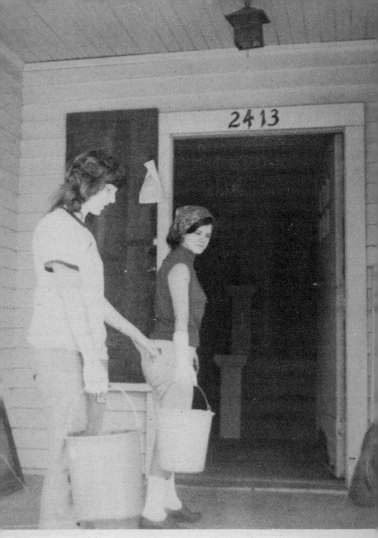

Girls' House cleanup

helped us meet the needed amount for the down payment. After all this, the woman who owned the house decided she didn't want to sell it.

In October, Carol again searched for more "For Sale" signs. She had me look at a large three-story, seven-bedroom house that had two balconies. The windows were broken, plaster was falling and there was no plumbing or heating.

I spoke to the mortgage company and they knocked $5,000 off the price. We could purchase it with nothing down and no payments for five months. Since it was the right size and the terms were reasonable, we referred to it from then on as a house with "great potential." Carol Zerbe, Carol Froese and two other girls moved into our "mansion," in January, 1973. A few days later Mary arrived to set up permanent housekeeping in this place where God had called her. There weren't enough beds. The first-floor windows were boarded up and the higher windows covered with sheets. There was only one bathtub. Mary never felt such deep depression. She found a suntan cot, put blankets under and over her and went to sleep.

Six o'clock the next morning. Carol Zerbe woke everyone up announcing that they had to get started painting. In two days five girls would be coming from Tabor to stay with them during another Urban Encounter. They'd work a while, then sit by the stove and drink hot tea and pray (and sometimes cry). Then they'd go back to work. This was repeated every few hours.

Finally the staff agreed they couldn't finish the painting in time anyhow, so they put five donated couches in one of the downstairs rooms, a rug in the middle of the floor and plugged in an electric heater. This is where the five visitors slept.

Painting the Girls' House

The girls from Tabor helped with the painting. People brought furniture. And the first month all the windows and sinks were installed, walls repaired and even a central heating system donated.

Stan Gordon became an important person to the girls living there. Stan called the World Impact office one day and said, "I'm a chemist, God told me to call you but I don't know why. Let me know if there's anything I can do for you." Where could we use a chemist?

When Stan came to the dedication of the Girls' House, he knew what his work was. He saw a hundred small jobs that needed to be done—a doorknob here, a screen door there, putty that window, etc. So every Saturday Stan comes and the girls always have a long list of jobs for him.

"Tell Them About Jesus"

Shortly after the girls had moved into the house, and were still busy with the remodeling, ten-year-old Mike dropped by.

Mary invited him and some of his friends to share a Valentine's cake. After they played some games, they sat in front of a roaring fire and the boys asked for a story. Mary told them about Daniel and his three friends in the fiery furnace. When Mike asked how he could live for God Mary told him, "Become a child of God." Mike and his friend Jamie prayed to receive Christ.

The boys wanted to study the Bible together, so while Mary got the Bible, Mike got more firewood. After the study, the boys wanted to be sure there would be more times like this. The next morning they came by at 8:00, to say "hi" and ask when they could come over again to study the Bible. The first two weeks Mike memorized three Bible verses.

Once Mike spent an entire day with Mary painting and talking about his past, his relatives and friends.

"I have twelve brothers and sisters. My oldest brother is in jail. He shot fifteen policemen with a machine gun."

"My sister's little girl, that's my niece, was shot. And so was my brother's best friend, Tony. He was twelve."

"My best friend, Bobby, was riding his bike and a drunk hit him with his car. Bobby was dragged for half a block and then he died."

Mike took Mary home to meet his mother. Later as he walked Mary back to the Girls' House he asked, "Mary, did you tell my mom about Jesus?"

"No, I didn't, Mike," Mary answered, "did you tell her?"

"No, I want you to tell her, you can do it better."

Soon Mike was bringing his friends over and saying, "Tell them about Jesus, Mary."

He brought Earl one day. Mike was worried about Earl, he was only eight years old, but seemed headed for a life of crime. He was being drawn into gang activity by the older boys.

As Mary was conducting the lesson, Mike kept interrupting to make sure Earl understood. Finally he asked Mary if she would stop so he could tell Earl something. He said, "Earl, you don't have to steal like you do. Jesus can clean you up and you can be a good boy."

Earl looked questioningly at Mary. "I don't know how."

Then Mike got on his knees and got Earl down beside him. "Just say what I say," he said, and Mike repeated the prayer Mary had prayed with him, "God, I'm sorry I've been so bad. Please forgive me and come into my life and be my Saviour." Earl repeated the prayer.

"There's more you should know, Earl," Mike added, "when you feel like doing bad things again, you have to ask God to help you not to do it. Then if you go ahead and do it anyhow, you have to ask forgiveness."

Mike told Earl about heaven with real enthusiasm. Earl laughed and clapped his hands and asked Mary, "Is it all right to be so excited?"

Mike asked, "Can my sisters come over?" Mary said, "Sure, we'd love to have them. Tell them to come to club next Wednesday."

After club, Mike asked Mary if Suzie, his eight-year-old sister had accepted Christ. When Mary answered, "I don't think she has." Mike said, "Well, why not?"

The next week Suzie told Mary she had prayed to receive Christ. Within a week Suzie brought four other girls who accepted Christ. Suzie was really excited.

Many inner city children identify discipline with anger and rejection. They are conditioned to believe that if they once disobey *and get caught,* they're no longer Christians. When Mary disciplined Suzie for breaking a rule of the Girls' House, Suzie looked up at Mary and asked, "I'm still your sister, ain't I?"

Bubbles, Bats, Brutality

One afternoon, several visitors were at the Girls' House when Earl and Mike came running up to the porch screaming and yelling.

"A man jumped Earl's mother," someone shouted. Everyone scaled the ten-foot fence, ran through the vacant lot and crossed the street to Earl's house.

As Mary and Carol arrived at Earl's house a score of kids were in the front yard. Cheryl Dorman, a staff member was limping up to the front door. (She dislocated her knee following the kids over the fence.)

Inside the house was Earl's mother Gloria, trying to

ward off the blows of a baseball bat wielded by her husband "Bubbles."

Bubbles yelled, "Get lost!" when he saw Cheryl at the door. None of the staff dared to go in. The children had convinced them that Bubbles had a gun and wasn't afraid to use it.

Earl and his three-year-old sister, also named Gloria, were running from the front porch to the gate crying. Mary picked up the frightened child and held her close. It was indeed a strange sight. Gloria screaming inside, obviously being beaten, and Mary holding little Gloria close and singing to her, trying to keep her from becoming hysterical. The child began to relax in Mary's arms. Mary hugged her tightly.

Meanwhile, Carol Froese ran to Mike's house and found Mike's mother calling the police.

The police are cautious of getting involved in domestic quarrels. When the unmarked patrol car drove by, it didn't stop until the officers saw the group congregated in the front yard. Then it backed up. The youngsters ran to the car and told the police what was happening. They didn't get out of the car until Carol Froese verified that a woman was being beaten.

"She's not screaming anymore," Carol said, "but she certainly has been."

"Who are you, a social worker?" they asked.

"No," she replied, "I just live here."

When the officers entered the house, there was a brief skirmish. A few minutes later, they brought the handcuffed husband out and took him away. Mary still held little Gloria.

After the patrol car was well out of sight, Carol went to the door to see if she could help.

Earl, with pleading eyes, said, "You can come in and talk to her if you want to. You can!"

Our staff and all the kids who had been at the Girls' House, went in and sat with the mother and her children.

Gloria had only been married to this man for a short time, but like her previous husband, he delighted in beating her. Earl, sitting next to his mom, just smiled and smiled at Mary. He told his mother all about Mary and said how happy he was that Mary lived close to him.

Later that evening Earl came to the Girls' House and happily informed them that Bubbles and his mother were back in bed together. Everything was all right.

Gloria's 15-year-old daughter, Pauline, is pregnant. When Bubbles tried to force Pauline into bed with him, Pauline's boyfriend shot and wounded him.

Continuous violence and immorality right in the home, forces me to wonder what the effect will be on the attitude of these children toward marriage and family life.

Robbed

Saturday, March 3, the Girls' House was empty all morning. The staff was involved in youth clubs and a special field trip. When Mary returned a little after noon she noticed the tin foil was out of the hole in the front door. She saw a small radio on the floor. She had a sick feeling in her stomach as she thought the house might have been robbed.

She was afraid to go into the house, but knew she had to. She looked for her cassette recorder, one of the most expensive things she had ever owned. It was gone. Kitchen cupboards were all open, drawers were pulled out and the window in the back door was broken. Mary thought, "I've got to keep cool. I've got to do the right thing."

80

She went upstairs and started from room to room. Her spirits sank deeper. Everything—record players, cameras, sewing machine, hair dryers, TV set, typewriters —everything of any value that could be moved, was gone.

She phoned the police and, shaking all over, told them what had happened. Then she sat down and cried. When she regained her composure, she phoned the PTL house and Thuan came right over.

She found the one old record player that had not been taken, and put on a record of a Bible reading of John 14. Thuan and Mary sat dejectedly, looked at each other and listened, "Let not your heart be troubled . . . in my Father's house are many mansions."

Before long, a seven-year-old boy named Les walked into the house. "Someone broke your back window," he blurted out. He described the culprit and Mary recognized him as Andy, a fellow who had been to the house a few days before.

When the police arrived, Mary answered questions for the better part of the afternoon. The officers asked Mary to get Les. Although she didn't want to involve any children, she got Les and brought him to the officers as casually as possible.

The police asked Mary, "Do you know any of the neighbors well enough to ask where Andy lives?"

Mary drove to the next street to Mike's house. Mike's father was on the front porch and she asked him if he'd seen anything. He said he had seen a gang of guys carrying a bunch of stuff out of the vacant lot, adjacent to the girls' back yard. He hadn't realized what they were doing.

While they were talking two guys walked up the street. "That's them," he yelled just as the police got there. The two guys stopped a passing car, hopped in and took off.

The police got the license number and radioed it in. Mary went home.

Les told Mary that Andy lived three blocks from the Girls' House. When Mary reported the address to the police she learned that they had already located the car at that same address. As the officers attempted to search the house, the parents fought to keep them out. They had to force their way in.

The father was arrested. In the confusion, the mother, several months pregnant, fell down the stairs. She claimed the police pushed her and later filed a lawsuit against the officers. The police took her to the hospital with an injured back.

Inside the house the police found fourteen-year-old Rick under the blankets. He was the leader of the gang that robbed the girls' bedroom. Rick was crying.

Rick and his friends already had a dozen charges against them including armed robbery, grand theft auto, and the illegal possession of drugs.

A year ago his twenty-year-old brother, Steven, cheated a man in gambling and was shot to death, around the corner from the Girls' House. Norm, his nine-year-old brother, watched the shooting. He was afraid to move because he thought he'd get shot too. As a result of Steven's death Rick became cruel and violent. Norm isn't afraid to move anymore. Now he runs with Rick. It's hard not to fear Rick's gang, but it's easy to see why he's so mean.

Robberies cause much turmoil in the minds of believers. Mary wrote to me shortly after the robbery: "I can't resolve it by saying, 'God took it because we really didn't need it,' as some Christians are saying in an attempt to console us. Cheryl, Carol and I all feel that we were using the tape recorders for clubs, the sewing machine for making curtains for the house and the typewriter for business. Therefore I don't feel it was God's will that they were stolen. The power of evil is strong in the community and the incident impresses us with the fantastic need in our neighborhood.

"It's been difficult for me to meet the guys who robbed us on the street or to see them run through our back yard. All the neighbor kids know who robbed us too. Three of our good teen-age girl friends, who come over often, were running around with them last weekend. There seems to be no conscience. It's weird too when brothers and sisters come over. In fact, some of the gang members have been in here since."

In the evening of March 14, two of Mike's older brothers dropped by several times looking for Rick and his gang. They were furious. Rick's gang had broken the back window in their father's car because he'd identified them to the girls and the police. Mike's brothers beat Rick badly when they found him, putting him in the hospital. That same night some of the gang attempted to set Mike's house on fire.

Mary was troubled that she had gotten Mike's family involved so she went to apologize. They told Mary that she could call on them any time for help. They expressed delight for what the girls were doing for their kids. Our staff has visited their home every Sunday since. Mary says, "I love them and their thirteen kids. I feel right at home."

Mike's father told Mary, "Rick's family is poor. They need to steal." He took Mary to his kitchen and with great pride, showed her a nine-cubic-foot deep freezer stuffed with packed meats and said, "See, *I* provide for *my* family." He showed her the cupboards and boasted that

83

his wife had canned most of that herself. Mike has an unusual father.

Attempted Rape

Celia is the twenty-four-year-old mother of four children. The two older ones continually drop by the Girls' House. One day Celia came to find out what they were doing. She told Mary that God somehow always brought her to Christians. She said she had accepted Christ when she was a child, but today she is an alcoholic, a drug user, and is separated from her husband.

Celia wanted Mary to teach her the Bible. When Mary called to pick her up, a week later, Celia wasn't there.

The following week, Celia dropped by the Girls' House. Her eyes were black and swollen. Two men had jumped into her car, beat her up and forced her to go to a motel with them with the intention of raping her. Because she was outnumbered and scared she decided to play along. They soon had her stripped naked. Thinking quickly she asked if she could go to the bathroom. Since it was cold she wrapped a sheet around her body.

On her way to the bathroom she noticed the outside door wasn't locked so she made a dash for it. Her assailants pursued her. They hit her over the head with a pop bottle and tried to drag her back. Celia managed to hang onto the open door. The maid walked by just then and helped her. Celia escaped, but the guys kept her car.

The next time Mary went to pick up Celia for a Bible study, she found two men, a woman, and Celia stoned in her apartment.

Two days later Celia asked Mary to keep her children for a few days because she had to go to jail. She was booked for fighting with her boyfriend and for possession of marijuana.

Mary cared for Celia's eight-month-old baby who was as small as a two-month-old child. Most of the time he just lay in a fetal position. He couldn't turn over or crawl. After a few days with the girls, he began to respond to their affection and cuddling, and he laughed out loud several times.

When Celia came for him, Mary asked her why she continued seeing her boyfriend since they had so many fights. Celia said, "You don't understand. I have to keep him. I need his money to keep my kids alive."

Doctors say that Celia is a hopeless case. She has almost destroyed her body with alcohol and drugs. Beyond that, it seems she has sunk so far that she can't even make a choice to accept God's grace. Celia is an example of thousands of young mothers in urban America who desperately need Christ but are so deep in sin that only a miracle can bring them to Him.

She's Not Worth Your Love

Becky the girl Mary met in Watts, attended club regularly after the summer of 1972. Becky seemed determined to give Mary trouble. She'd bring her friends to club just to cause a disturbance. One day she tore up some of the crafts that the younger children had made. Mary was annoyed and told her not to come if she was only there to cause trouble. Later Mary was warned by a "little messenger" that Becky was going to beat her up. The next week in club Becky slugged Mary once and then looked embarrassed when Mary didn't react.

Becky stayed away for a long time. One day she showed up with a gang of guys to disturb Mary's class. They stood

Mary Thiessen and Bible class

right in front of Mary when she was leading the children in singing.

Becky lost interest again and didn't come to club for weeks. She showed up one day, walked right up to Mary and asked for her phone number. Mary thought, "Oh, boy, threatening calls, just what I need." But she gave it to her anyhow, and Becky began to call her every day.

She again asked, "How do I become a Christian?" She'd talk to different girls in the house and ask them how they got saved and what they had done before. She was trying to find out if it were possible for someone like herself to live a Christian life. When the girls would press her, she'd say, "I'm not ready yet."

One Wednesday night she came to a pajama party at the Girls' House and experienced real Christian fellowship and fun. She loved that night and didn't want to go home. She hugged Mary and wouldn't let her go.

The next evening we had a board meeting at the Girls' House. When the phone rang it was Becky asking to speak to Mary. She told Mary she had a fight with her mother and had taken pills. Mary asked, "How many?" She said, "Guess." So they played a guessing game and Mary finally found out she had taken twenty aspirins. Mary called her doctor and he said she should be taken to an emergency ward of a hospital.

Mary and Sue Swain went to Becky's house. Becky was beginning to feel sick but was afraid for Mary to tell her mother what she had done. Mary had to get Becky's mother's signature on a parental permission form before the hospital would admit Becky. Her mother had been drinking and didn't want to be bothered signing a release. When the girls finally told Mrs. Wilson that Becky had taken an overdose, she was furious and told Becky, "I hate you."

At the hospital the girls saw a very meek, scared Becky who begged them to stay with her. Sue and Mary walked the halls with her and held her hands while she got rid of what was inside through induced vomiting. She asked the girls to pray for her out loud. They did. Then Becky prayed out loud and thanked God for Mary and Sue.

After she prayed she told them that she had asked Christ to come into her life at the pajama party.

Becky had to have an injection. She cried and said she was afraid of needles. Mary prayed that God would help Becky be brave. God definitely answered prayer and Becky took the needle showing very little fear.

When her mother arrived to sign more papers, she refused to talk to Becky. She turned away from her when Becky cried, "Mama, mama!" and said, "You don't need me."

Mary followed her out of the room and said, "I'm so sorry all of this has happened, we love Becky and feel badly for her."

Mrs. Wilson told Mary, "Don't you be bothering with Becky, she's not worth your love."

When Becky's sister came to visit her she said, "I wish you'd died."

Becky stayed in the hospital two days longer than necessary because her mother refused to sign the release. When she did go home, her mother wouldn't speak to her for days. Their first communication was a fight.

A few weeks later Becky led three of her friends to Christ. She was thrilled. It's hard to be a follower of Christ in the ghetto.

Becky was a new Christian. Her faith was tested immediately, her brother was arrested for stealing; her thirteen-year-old friend died from a blood clot during pregnancy. Becky saw a group of dudes jump a white cab driver. She picked up his car key and took him to a phone. Her own brother beat her up badly because she helped a white man. Her sister was stabbed by a boyfriend. Her brother's father died last week. (He was one of the many men her mother had been married to.) Becky doesn't know who her father is. No one really seems to know. Her mother is a confirmed alcoholic. Her sister is a pusher.

Becky is growing in Christ, but sin gets her down. After Bible study, she often begs everyone to pray for her. Sometimes she says, "It's impossible to be a Christian in the housing projects. I wish I could die."

CHAPTER
SIX

NEW WORK IN WICHITA

In the winter of 1969 I studied at Fuller Seminary and continued my ministry in Watts. One morning at school I received a message asking me to return a call to Dr. Roy Just at Tabor College, a Mennonite school in Hillsboro, Kansas. I thought it was a joke! I never heard of Tabor College, or Hillsboro, Kansas, and I pictured Mennonites as old-fashioned people: women in long dresses and no makeup; men with beards and funny hats.

But I had nothing to lose since the note said to call "collect." I dialed the operator and gave her the information. My suspicions increased when the Newton, Kansas operator said, "I have no idea where Hillsboro is, I never heard of it." Five minutes later, however, her supervisor found the routing to Hillsboro and connected me with Roy Just, president of Tabor College.

He invited me to preach at the commencement exercises of their graduating class that May. This resulted in an invitation from Roy to start an urban ministry in Wichita, Kansas, fifty miles from the college, using Tabor students as youth club leaders.

Roy wrote to the entire student body telling of the opportunity to serve in urban Wichita and encouraging those interested to attend the orientation classes that I would conduct in September.

The project was committed to God. We prayed for twenty-five college students to participate in the youth club program, and found three appropriate locations where we could hold the clubs.

We could only guess how the Tabor students would respond. When the orientation session convened, instead of twenty-five applicants, we had closer to sixty.

I talked to them frankly, encouraging the unfaithful to drop out of the program. I warned that the project required a time investment of every Saturday morning and a 100-mile drive. Four dropped out.

A Slow Beginning

When I interviewed Al Ewert at the fall training session he said, "After reading Dr. Just's letter, I was convinced I wanted to be part of this new outreach. I mailed my response the same day to make sure I would be selected. Many times this past summer," he added, "I wondered whether I am the type of person who is able to relate to inner city people."

I decided Al was the type, and asked him to be one of the core leaders. He was excited about the opportunity, but surprised at being selected. God has an amazing way of pointing out potential workers to me. I prayed about Al and was certain that he was the man for the job.

The first day that Al met with the ten college students in his core, everyone, including Al, was nervous. They were assigned to the Mexican-American area, Waco-Finn. They wondered what that first day would be like.

On Saturday morning, the Tabor students gathered for prayer before starting the hour's drive to Wichita. They were excited but insecure. When they arrived at Waco-Finn, there were very few children on the streets. They wondered if there were any kids in the area or if they were still asleep. Al divided the collegians into pairs, one guy and one girl, and sent them on a door-to-door canvass of the neighborhood to recruit children for the youth club. They found many children and invited them all to come.

After an hour of canvassing, the whole group returned to the church and waited for the children. Very few showed up. The collegians encouraged each other with, "Next week we'll have a big crowd."

The following Saturday Al took his group to Waco-Finn again. Again they canvassed the area and met with the same response. This time there was visible dis-

Estelle House staff men

couragement among the core members, although no one verbalized it. Tabor students in other areas had been met with outstretched arms as scores of kids joined the youth clubs. But Waco-Finn had only a few. There were more college students than children.

Al was discouraged as we talked after the third Saturday. "I'd like to be completely honest with you, Keith."

"Go ahead, Al, tell me exactly what's on your heart."

"Some of the kids in my core feel we should abandon Waco-Finn and look for a new area. Some suggest we work with other cores who have too many kids to handle."

"What's your opinion?"

Al thought for a moment, "I've put in too much time and prayer to quit. But I admit that only having three kids today is depressing."

"I know. Why do you think there are so few coming out?"

"It's a strong Catholic community. I think that our meeting in the Quaker church is the main reason. There are no strong feelings against our being white."

We talked for a while longer. I was sure he was thinking, "Boy, this is a waste of time." The excitement of the new inner city project that promised glamorous victories for God like those in *The Cross and the Switchblade*, had worn mighty thin for Al. I encouraged him as much as I could. Al responded by challenging his core group that week to pray more for specific things. One definite thing they prayed for was that twenty-five to thirty Mexican-American kids would come to club regularly. They felt God's presence and were sure that He would begin blessing them. The next Saturday morning their faithfulness was blessed with fifteen children at youth club, half of them Mexican-Americans. Each week the numbers increased and within a month God answered their prayer with thirty Mexican-Americans regularly attending the weekly Bible club.

Day on the Farm

The involvement of the Tabor students with the children the first year went far beyond weekly clubs. One hundred youngsters came from Wichita to Hillsboro for Tabor's homecoming football game. Some sat on the sidelines with the players. Others came to Tabor for parties and plays. Some children spent the night with their club leaders on the college campus. Relationships were established that carry over until today.

One of Al's projects was to take the city kids to a farm for a day. Thirty were in the first group. They climbed into five cars. Al poked his head into each car and said, "When we get to the farm, don't jump out and run around; stay in groups and wait until I tell you what to do." They all seemed to understand.

There was such excitement enroute that no one sat still. When they arrived, the thirty kids took off in thirty different directions. Some scared the cows, others chased the chickens. They were in the pigpen, petting the pigs and falling in the mud. Some of the little ones stood still and cried in all the confusion.

Al had a great impulse to laugh, but swallowed hard. He was afraid the farmer was angry about the assault on his animals. When he saw the farmer "cracking up" at the sight, Al laughed too. For the first hour they let the kids run wherever they wanted to.

The noon wiener roast was characterized by fights over Kool-Aid, catsup-covered kids and more mud. That afternoon the farmer hitched a trailer to his tractor and took

Vern Cole and children, on an outing

them for a ride through a dry creek bed and across his pasture so that the kids could see some calves that were born the day before.

Later he saddled some horses and the braver children went horseback riding.

These youngsters, who had seldom been out of the city, never forgot this day. The staff built strong relationships through outings like this.

The Rubalcabas

When I encouraged the staff to begin an adult Bible study, Al reacted, "I'll do it, but I don't feel qualified."

They went out in pairs and surveyed the area to determine the interest. In six homes people expressed a desire for such a study. They set a date and Al spent a week preparing.

He and Bev Miller, a summer volunteer, arrived at the church a half hour early. They were as nervous as infantrymen in a mine field. After an hour of waiting, no one came. Al calmed down—relieved but disappointed. He knew the Bible study was God's will!

The next two Wednesday nights the same thing happened even though they had called at each home and sent postcards to remind them of the day of the study. Finally they decided if no one came the following week, they would look for another area.

No one showed up and they were discouraged. As they were leaving the church, they met Mr. Valdez, an elderly man who had stopped by the church many times during youth club.

Sensing his sympathetic spirit, Al and Bev poured out their problem to him.

"Perhaps God sent me at the right time," he said. "I know a family who lives near and will be glad to come."

Quickly Al took the name, "Rubalcaba."

"My wife had a Bible study with the mother of the family," said Mr. Valdez. "When you go to their house tell them that I sent you."

That night Al met the entire Rubalcaba family: Mr. Rubalcaba, who had worked at Cessna Aircraft for fifteen years, Mrs. Rubalcaba and Lupe, 15, Juanita, 14 and Jose, 13. They agreed to have the Bible study in their home.

The following Wednesday night, Al and Bev drove into Waco-Finn for the fifth week in a row. Mrs. Rubalcaba greeted them at the door and called her entire family into the front room. Everyone nervously waited for the others who had promised to come. Small talk was difficult.

Soon Mr. Valdez came with a woman. Al conducted a general study of the Bible, since the group had almost no knowledge of it. Even though they were "religious" people, they had no idea what a book of the Bible was, let alone chapters or verses. They didn't know there was an old and new testament. They asked Al where different stories were found. The Rubalcabas were so excited with the Genesis account of creation, that their chatter drifted into Spanish.

The next week Al took paperback New Testaments and everyone bought one for a quarter. With each person having the same version they began a study of John. Each one read a verse out loud. Sometimes the children helped Mr. Rubalcaba with the pronunciation of an English word. Everyone enjoyed it.

The group met every week that summer. When Bev returned to Seattle, Al continued the study. It was the highlight of his week. Often he'd talk with the three teenagers even after the parents had gone to bed.

I Can't Dance

In Mexico a girl's fifteenth birthday is cause for a big celebration. Often there is a week of parties and gifts are brought by relatives and close friends. For months the Rubalcabas planned Juanita's coming out party. Al's intimate relationship with the family was demonstrated by his invitation to the entire affair. Al sang at the mass in the morning, and was an honored guest at the dinner for 200,

98

and the formal ball in the evening at the huge civic center, "Century II."

The ballroom was decorated with pink and blue streamers which came together to form a big heart with "Juanita" written across it. The 500 guests grew quiet as the band began to play and Juanita came in, followed by her ten attendants dressed in pink and blue formals. Al realized more and more that the Rubalcabas were very influential in the Mexican community.

Everyone formed a large circle as Mr. Rubalcaba was the first to dance with Juanita. After Lupe danced with her, the floor was open and everyone started to dance. Al's heart sank when he saw Mrs. Rubalcaba motioning for him to dance with her. He shook his head, "No." She laughed and said, "Come on, Al, dance with me."

Al had never danced in his life but walked bravely out on the floor and made an effort to do what everyone else did. Mr. Rubalcaba laughed. Lots of people were watching. Al was relieved when the music stopped.

A place was reserved for Al at the family table. He knew people wondered what he was doing there, especially after they saw him dance.

"I learned a lesson from this," Al told me, "that affected my ministry. It is one thing to be involved with people in a Bible study, but if that's your only involvement in their lives, it's a shallow relationship. After that one evening, I wasn't just their Bible teacher, I was a part of their total lives. The Bible studies were much more open. I was invited to meals and to visit friends and relatives with them. It is a beautiful relationship."

The Field

By the end of the first year Al was a friend with many

older teen-agers. In August he invited three guys to go camping with him, Michael and Lonzo who were brothers, and Lupe Rubalcaba.

They arrived at a lake fifty miles from Wichita early in the morning and pitched their tent. It was still cool outside when Lupe said, "Hey, let's go swimming."

That was the last thing Al wanted to do, but he said, "Sure, why not?" As they plunged into the cold water, Al prayed, "Lord, I'll do anything they want within reason, just help me develop a close friendship with these guys and become a part of their lives."

They spent the day swimming, fishing and hiking. When dusk fell they piled into Al's car for a ride around the lake. As they drove by a cornfield Al remembered how much fun it was to run through the rows of corn. He stopped the car, jumped out and without a word to the guys, tore through the field.

Since it was getting dark and they were "out of their turf" the fellows took off after him. Al was well into the field, but he heard them yelling, "Al! Al! You're crazy! Al!" He stopped and lay down between the rows so they couldn't see him. When he heard them panting and getting close, he jumped up, shaking the corn. They screamed and laughed and then gave him a few friendly shoves and jabs.

As they walked back toward the car, the guys thought Al was really cool. It was dark by now and they were ready to leave. Just when they began to feel safe, Al took off again, dodging in and out of the rows. This time they didn't follow him, but found their way back to the car. Michael and Lonzo got into the car, but Lupe stood on top of it so he could see the corn shake as Al walked through the rows. He reported to the guys in the car.

Al waited fifteen minutes, crawled through the high grass along the road and jumped out yelling and screaming. Their reaction to Al's return was one of fear mixed with joy.

After barbecued hamburgers, the guys crawled into their sleeping bags because it was cold. Michael, the youngest, was afraid and wanted to sleep as close to Al as possible.

Al told the fellows they would have devotions every night and a special church service on Sunday morning. By the light of a small lantern, Al told them the story of Daniel in the lion's den and how he was saved because he trusted God. Al explained how each of them needed to trust God in the same way. They could do that by asking Jesus to take first place in their lives.

As he explained the plan of salvation, he realized that this was the first time in the three months he had known these guys that they understood what he was trying to communicate.

"God is giving each of you a chance to become a Christian tonight," he said, "I'm going to pray a prayer out loud and if you want to invite Jesus into your life, you pray the same words silently to God."

When he finished praying, he said, "If you prayed that prayer, tell me about it tonight or in the morning."

They were quiet and wanted to go to sleep. But before Michael went to sleep, he told Al he had become a Christian. Michael meant business, and as Al dozed off to sleep he thought, "All these months of work are worth it even if Michael is the only one."

The next morning they couldn't find Lupe anywhere. During the two-hour search, Lonzo confided in Al that he became a Christian the night before.

Lupe strolled back into camp, his fishpole over his shoulder. He hadn't caught any fish, but he was proud that he had gotten up before the others and gone fishing by himself. He obviously wanted to do some thinking alone.

While the other two were busy cleaning up, Lupe said to Al, "I prayed that prayer with you last night and accepted Christ as my Saviour. This is a new way to me, Al. I want to talk to my family about it and to the priest to make sure it's all right."

The boys returned to Wichita and told everyone about running through the cornfield. A year later they still talked about "their cornfield", and their good friend, Al. Everyone wanted to be Al's friend.

Estelle Street

I prayed for a live-in house in Wichita for over a year, so I was excited when a group of Christian businessmen invited me to share the work with them. They wanted to help me pray for this live-in ministry. When I arrived at the office of George Fooshe, he led me to a small conference room in the rear where six businessmen met every Tuesday afternoon to pray for each other specifically and local ministries in general.

One after another, each man was led by the Holy Spirit to pray that God would provide World Impact with a facility in urban Wichita before I left town. I was scheduled to leave Wichita two and a half days later. George taped their prayers so that others could be encourgaed by God's answers.

We had invited a group of local ministers to lunch the following day to inform them about the goals and work of World Impact. George Wood, pastor of the Central Christian Church in Wichita, hosted the luncheon in a local restaurant. One of the last persons to arrive was a woman. I hadn't heard of any women pastors in the area and so I assumed she had wandered into the wrong room. No one had the heart to tell her to leave.

I shared our ministry. The pastors asked questions. Their warm response pleased me. I told them we were looking for a house in Wichita. I expected one of these men to put his arm around me and say, "God bless you, Keith, we believe in your work and my church will give you the money for your house." One by one they all approached me, put their arms around me and said, "God bless you, we believe in your work," and left. But no one offered us a house. They all left, except the woman.

She was radiant and couldn't contain her excitement. "My name is Lemoine Ralston, and I think I was led to this meeting by God."

Then she bubbled over, "I've got the house you've been praying for, and you can have it."

Less than a day after six businessmen claimed a house for God's kingdom in urban Wichita, He provided it.

When Al first saw the house on Estelle Street and met Lemoine and her husband, Loren, it was obvious the one house was too small for the envisioned ministry. The house next door had been a "good time" house; a combination nightclub and house of prostitution, until it was closed by police the year before. The Ralstons' church agreed to pay the rent on the second house. So we started our Wichita live-in ministry with two small homes next door to each other.

When Al and three other men moved into Estelle, they were warmly received by scores of children. Youth clubs and Sunday School were well attended.

When Al and his staff first moved into the Estelle houses

they were awakened every night by a bunch of teen-agers—the community's official welcoming committee. They'd knock on the windows and yell, or throw firecrackers into the house or pitch a bucket of water which soaked Al, the floor, the bed and the whole room. The summer staff kept good-natured about it feeling it was a small sign of their acceptance.

There were fourteen on summer staff when a ten-member musical group arrived for ten days. There was still no furniture in the houses and only cold running water. There was no refrigerator, but Al jokingly says, "Since we had no food and very little money, there wasn't much need for a refrigerator.

"We could only laugh. And we did plenty of it. The more problems we had the funnier they seemed. The big joke was about food. Once we had hamburger patties. The girls only had one pound of hamburger so they put lots of flour, corn flakes and who knows what else in them. We agreed that it was a good thing they were so small because if they had been big enough to see, no one would have eaten them.

"One day we had soup and cheese sandwiches and we each got a half cup of soup and half of a sandwich."

No one complained. Praising the Lord for everything was the order of the day. It was a precious lesson in faith for everyone.

Transformation

We met Ken through one of our junior high youth clubs. Ken lives with two brothers, five sisters and two cousins. Fighting was his favorite pastime, as his scarred body verifies.

Ken didn't like to steal much, but occasionally lifted ice cream because everyone else was doing it. His language reflected the streets; his parents didn't care. As a child he frequently attended church with his grandmother, who was usually drunk in the services. Ken's parents didn't like church, and neither did he, except for the cookies and Kool-Aid served there.

Trouble started for Ken in the seventh grade when the junior high school he attended began integration. Fights broke out at school every day. Ken felt the principal was prejudiced against blacks. When a white boy pushed Ken against the gym door, Ken retaliated by knocking out his opponent's front teeth. The principal and teachers ran to the fight. Ken fled, leaving the fellow lying on the floor.

The principal threatened Ken with expulsion if he ever hurt anyone like that again, even if it wasn't his fault. Ken relates: "Black kids get kicked out of school for doing less than that white kid did to me."

Soon Ken joined a black gang dedicated to fighting white kids. By student agreement the school halls were divided between black and white students. The whites never dared to step on the black side. But the blacks felt perfect liberty to walk on the white side—nothing ever happened to them. The blacks jumped on anyone who made an ugly face or said something offensive. Ken was kicked out of the seventh grade three times for fighting. He initiated fights, so white kids would get kicked out, too.

Because of fighting, Ken was transferred to another integrated junior high for the eighth grade. Trouble started there during a football game between blacks and whites. A white guy tackled Ken and took the ball away. Ken slugged the white fellow, knocked him down and kicked him repeatedly. Ken was expelled from school for a week.

Ken threatened his music teacher with a drum stick "because he was prejudiced." He was suspended for obscenity. Finally, he was expelled for the remainder of the school year when he called his English teacher an "old bitch."

One thing Ken liked better than fighting was to isolate a white girl on the school stairs and "feel her up." Ken relates, "The girls didn't like it, but never reported me, so I never got caught." He quit when his black friends called him an "Uncle Tom" for this activity.

106

Ken's life changed direction when he accepted Christ during a junior high camping trip. Fernando, a World Impact staff member, told Ken he needed to study the Word and walk closely with God. Ken met every Monday with Fernando to study the Bible and discuss the junior high club program. Spiritual growth was obvious. When school started Fernando's junior high club elected Ken as their leader.

Ken wanted to tell his friends about Jesus but he was afraid and didn't know how to approach them. His opportunity came in his speech class. He spoke about Christianity. He thanked Fernando for telling him that Christ wasn't afraid to die on the cross for him, so why should he fear sharing Christ with others. He spoke about his life and his new attitude toward school and teachers because of Christ. He got an "A" on the speech.

Ken's life indeed changed. He doesn't fight at home any more. Visiting relatives ask why he is so different from his brother, who was expelled from school three times in one semester.

Barbecued Bologna

In fall Al planned a neighborhood barbecue to bring the community closer together. The high school youth helped plan the barbecue and took the leadership in conducting it. One hundred fifty people came to the Sunday afternoon event. They blocked off the street and had an hour of games for all ages, including a tug-of-war and mother-daughter balloon stomp.

After the street games everyone moved in between the two houses for the meal, which featured barbecued bologna. This was followed by a program in the backyard led by the Sunday School class. There was group singing, skits and a devotional time. People were exposed to the claims of Christ in what we hoped would be an annual affair.

Praise God for the Broken Window

The ministry matured; youth clubs and Bible studies grew. But Al was bothered by the lack of communication with the 16- to 20-year olds. Little was being done for them. Al prayed for God to raise up ten to fifteen black men who could be discipled during the following year. He prayed they would meet together for regular Bible study as a direct step towards finding Christ and becoming disciples.

One night a group of older guys played a few games of Ping-Pong at our house. Donald accidentally broke a window. They left immediately.

When Al arrived about a half hour later, a group of children rushed to Al reporting that Donald broke the window. They wanted to see some action and pointed to Donald standing across the street with a gang of fellows. Al saw these guys often and had tried to initiate contact with them, but they were always cold.

Al's first inclination was not to go across the street, but he knew he should. He went inside the house and prayed, "Lord, when I go, I pray that Donald will be open and want to talk to me."

Nervously he walked to where the fellows were standing. Everyone watched to see what would happen. He approached Donald and said, "Hi, I'm Al."

Donald was embarrassed, "Man, I'll pay for it," he said.

"No problem. That's not why I came over. I wanted to get to know you dudes."

The others became uninterested and wandered off. Al

108

sensed that Donald was the only one who wasn't drunk or high.

"Are you still in school, Donald?"

"Yeah, I'm still in school. I stick with it because I like to play football."

"Great, are you on the team?"

"Yeah, but my real goal is college football."

Al surveyed Donald's stature, about 6 feet, 200 pounds.

"You look like you've got what it takes to make it. Do you like school?"

"No."

"Do you play any basketball?"

"No, just street ball. I never played basketball at school."

"Would you be interested in playing if we got a team together?"

"Sure, we used to play basketball in your backyard before you moved in. Did you play in college?"

"No, just in high school. Come by tomorrow and we'll play some ball."

"O.K."

"It was sure nice meeting you, Donald. Check with you later."

Al walked back to the house praising God with each step. Even though the conversation was short, he knew something would come of it. It took a long time for him to fall asleep that night, he couldn't praise God enough for the broken window. He remembered his prayer for a group of black men who could be discipled this year.

After the basketball team was underway, Al knew ten fellows very well. They came by the house every night and stayed late. One night at about 2:00 A.M. he said, "I think it's time we all got some sleep, but before you go, this

Thursday night we're going to have a Bible study here and I want you all to attend."

Everyone laughed.

"No, don't laugh, I'm serious. You guys are here every night anyhow and I expect you to come on Thursday." Then he asked each one personally if he would come. Each one said he would.

Wednesday night before the study one dude stuck his head back in the door as he was leaving and asked, "Say, man, we got to dress up for that study tomorrow?"

"No, I don't care how you're dressed, just that you come."

Al had no idea what to expect. They might laugh through the whole thing. He was concerned that the study relate to them, but he didn't want to water down the salvation message in any way.

In the afternoon a dude came by, "Are we still having that study?"

"Sure!"

That evening they were all there fifteen minutes early. They were nervous and found their seats quickly. Al looked at some of the wildest kids in the neighborhood, but they were quiet—even a little lonely.

He passed out Bibles to each one and Jack said, "Man, we gotta read?"

"You bet, everyone will read a paragraph and we'll go around the room. Open your Bibles to John 3."

Blank looks on each face.

"Open to page 199."

They read (or stumbled) through the whole chapter with Al helping them read so often that he wondered if anything was coming through.

There was dead silence until someone pronounced a

word poorly and then there was some snickering. They always shut each other up when that got out of hand.

When they had finished Al asked them simple questions like, "When did Nicodemus come to Jesus?"

Then he progressed to questions with a spiritual application. "What does it mean to be born again?"

As he explained he realized the Holy Spirit was breaking through. Then he asked a question that took everyone off guard, "How many of you guys think you're Christians?"

After a short silence, they all put up their hands. Then Jack put his head down and said, "I ain't no Christian. I'm bad. I'm bad. There ain't no way that I can be a Christian." He sat with his head in his hands.

Al continued. "Why do the rest of you believe that God should let you into heaven?"

No one said a thing. It was very quiet.

"Does it make any difference to any of you at all if you go to heaven or not?"

Jack said, "Yeah, man, if it keeps me from going down there (pointing downward) I want to know."

Al said, "Jack, it's a whole lot more than knowing whether or not you are going down there. Becoming a Christian means giving God your life by saying, 'Jesus, You take over. I know I'm bad but I want You to be in control of my life.' You can't stop sinning by yourself, but God can help you do it. He wants you to let Him take over your life. This means your entire life and not just a part of it. And it means for the rest of your life and not just for one evening.

"It's a gut-level thing, living the Christian life, it's no pansy existence." Al paused for a few seconds and then added, "Any of you guys ready for this kind of life?"

It was silent for a time and then Steve said, "Man, I'm ready." Next Derek, "I'm ready too." Then Jessie, "Me too."

Al paused again and said, "Anyone else ready?" Every guy's head was bowed, staring at the floor. There was no talking or laughing. By this time, Charlie Esters, a black Christian had come into the house. He took Jessie to the corner of the room.

As Al talked to Steve and Derek he saw Charlie and Jessie get on their knees. Right in front of the other guys, Jessie invited Jesus to come into his life. Al took Steve and Derek into another room and went through a few verses in Romans with them and then they each prayed.

Derek prayed, "God, I know I'm bad and messed up on a whole lot of people, but I want to change. Come into me and change me, and uh, that's all."

They read verses on assurance. Then Al asked, "Derek, if you were to die tonight where would you go?"

Without a pause, Derek answered, "Man, I'm going to heaven. Man, I'm going to heaven." Then he laughed. They all laughed and Al felt a joy like he had never experienced before. It blew his mind, God did more than he ever anticipated.

In the other room it was still quiet; no one was talking and the guys were nervous. Some walked around, went to the phone, picked it up, put it back down. Some picked up magazines, put them down.

Al talked to some of them. They were convicted, but weren't ready yet. At 1:00 A.M. everyone was still there. Derek and Steve memorized their first verses of Scripture and talked about the people they were going to tell about becoming Christians. Derek and Steve stayed all night and eventually moved in.

Before the rest left, Rodney said to Al, "When we gonna have another study?"

"Why don't we plan one for every Thursday evening?" Al suggested.

"No, man, let's have one tomorrow."

Al wasn't prepared for that, but said, "Sure."

Since these first three accepted Christ, twenty-five other dudes have made the same decision. Al maintains that watching a dude become a Christian is exciting, but the real thrill is seeing him mature into a man of God.

CHAPTER

SEVEN

HEALTHY AND GROWING AND FULL OF LOVE

Eighteen-year old Derek, a new believer, is one of eight children. When he was growing up he never got along with his family or at the Catholic elementary school he attended because he stole, fought, used weed, LSD, pills and speed.

Derek committed his first major offense when he was in the seventh grade. He and Vern Cole broke into an auto supply store in downtown Wichita late one Saturday night. They ripped off BB guns and an assortment of other small things.

Forced integration of his junior high school led to daily fights between blacks and whites. Derek was always involved. He loved to fight, and fighting resulted in a deep prejudice against whites. When Derek was fifteen, one day he walked down a school hallway and a white boy pushed him against a locker. Derek's well-known temper flared. He threw the boy in a locker and landed one blow after the other, finally hitting him with his cake cutter.

The boy, severely injured, was taken to a hospital; Derek was charged with assault and battery. Because witnesses saw the white boy start the fight, the charges against Derek were dropped. But the incident led to Derek's being expelled from school for the rest of the year. After that, he was repeatedly kicked out of school for fighting, until he finally quit school completely.

During Derek's school years, basketball was the main outlet for his energies. When he dropped out of school for good and started running the streets there was nothing in his life to deter him from trouble. During an eighteen-month period, Derek illegally entered fifteen stores and schools. He was never caught in these breaking and entering incidents, so he was never jailed.

Derek and Vern burglarized the auto supply store, again, and took more than fifty rifles, shotguns and pistols. Even though they were on bicycles, they successfully carried the goods back to their homes. They gave most of the guns away, keeping a few for their own collection.

Derek and two friends ripped off several hundred dollars' worth of leather coats. When the store manager gave chase and caught Derek, Derek beat the manager mercilessly, and the three youths escaped with the coats.

Derek and Vern were involved in an incident that sparked several weeks of rioting in Wichita. After an all-black high school lost a football game, twenty blacks stood outside the stadium. When several white boys tried to walk through the middle of the pack, the black boys jumped on them. Soon fighting was directed at the police. The blacks fled to the school grounds where the number

115

exploded to 150. Derek and Vern were there with a friend who had a large gun. When the riot helicopter flew over they shot it down. Derek was arrested. The police tried to stuff him into an already full paddy wagon—everyone burst out. Derek was finally apprehended and put on probation.

In the summer of 1972, Derek was at a party that the police raided. His friends were taken to jail. Derek got the license number of the squad car. Later in the week he saw the same car parked at a restaurant. He placed several railroad torches under the gas tank and blew up the police vehicle.

At one time Derek's mother put a revolver to his head and vowed she would kill him if she ever saw him again.

Derek was living on the streets. He went to the Estelle House for the first time to use the phone, and started dropping by regularly. The morning after he accepted Christ at the Thursday Bible Study, he shared with his friends that he had become a Christian. Mouths hung open. Everyone wanted to know what had happened.

Derek took an immediate stand for Christ, memorizing Scripture and telling his friends about Christ. Soon others followed him through the doors of Estelle House and into the arms of Christ.

Al wants to see constant growth in the new Christians instead of intermittent fleshly reversions. Many of them test his patience. But Al knows that the Lord never gives up on anyone, and He expects us to have this same patience with His children. Al needed much patience with Derek.

A group of kids started trouble at a youth center. Derek was there, but was not involved. When the police arrived they ordered everyone out of the building. One officer shoved Derek against the wall and Derek's hot temper reasserted itself; he knocked the policeman on the side of the head with a pool cue. Derek spent the day in jail but was released when witnesses claimed he was shoved for no reason.

Al spent hours talking to Derek about his temper. When he is calm, Derek realizes his temper can only lead him into trouble, but it's hard to remember when he is upset. Although he is not large, guys twice his size run when Derek loses his temper. He has quite a reputation—he seldom gets whipped.

Derek wants to direct this spare energy for the Lord. He often shares his testimony in local churches. He asked to go along when Al went to talk to a group of elderly women who support our house ministry by providing pillows and blankets. The two of them sang a couple of songs for the ladies. Derek, this black man who seldom associated with whites, really wanted to show his love for these elderly women. Just twelve months before he would have hated these same ladies, and might have tried to snatch their purses. Now he wanted to sing for them of Jesus and His love.

Grady

Grady's father died when he was three years old. His mother immediately remarried, which led to many problems in his family of five brothers and two sisters. Grady's older brothers ran away, were involved in fights and got kicked out of school. One brother is currently doing ten to twenty years in the penitentiary for burglary and manslaughter.

Grady started shoplifting when he was young but he was never arrested. When he was fourteen, he got a

117

twelve-year old girl pregnant and barely escaped being jailed. Then he had a fight with an older man and hit him in the throat with an iron pole. This time he was given a four-month jail term.

When he was released on probation, Grady got another girl pregnant. He was sentenced to the Boy's Industrial School for a year then placed in a half-way house.

Grady began attending the Tuesday night Bible study at Estelle House, and soon gave his life to Christ. The day after his conversion he told his girl friends about his new experience the night before. The girls looked at him in unbelief and laughed out loud. Grady didn't care. He was in love with Christ!

Because of his home situation, Grady moved into Estelle House. He was afraid that he would kill his stepfather if he lived at home. He soon became a keen student of the Word. Once, Fernando was talking with the men about the "end times." Grady, who had read a little about the book of Revelation, shared with the others what he understood the tribulation would be like.

He graphically described the lake of hell-fire and brimstone, emphasizing the perpetual heat the doomed would experience. As Grady named each man's sins for him, the potential punishment became more than his listeners could stand. One young man, Mike, was so scared that he yelled at Grady, "Stop talking about the 'revolution.'"

Grady wouldn't stop. Mike started to jump him but ran out of the house instead. Fernando watched him sprint down the street as fast as he could go. A few weeks later Mike was again invited to stay for the evening Bible study. Mike said he couldn't and just before Bible study he started to leave. Grady shoved him to the couch and said,

118

"Man, you're staying!"

Mike asked, "Are we going to talk about the 'revolution'?"

"Not tonight," Al replied.

Mike stayed. That night he found the Lord.

Eric

Eric Sorenson was a good student in grade school, but when he was bussed to a junior high out of his neighborhood, trouble followed. He fought every day. He was so bad that he looked forward to school just so he could fight some more. In his sophomore year of high school he was in eleven fights. Six times during the year he was kicked out of school for three days.

He cooled off somewhat in his junior year when he transferred to another high school and joined the wrestling team. Through athletics he made some white friends, so his feelings toward whites improved.

During the summer Eric played basketball at our house regularly. Around Christmas he and his seventeen year old brother, Carl, moved into our house. Eric and Carl were kicked out of their house and were running the streets. Their mother asked if they could move in with us. Their father, a wino, would beat their mother regularly and Eric would try to defend her by fist-fighting with him.

Eric and Carl lived with us for a month. They attended Bible study and took part in the activities of the house. Much prayer was uttered for their salvation, but they weren't ready. Then suddenly on February 6, both of them accepted the Lord. Al couldn't understand why Eric was so ready at that time. Two days later we found out that he had gotten a sixteen-year-old runaway girl pregnant. She had no relatives in Wichita and was completely alone.

Eric understood the forgiveness of God which became his when he became His child; he also recognized that he is still responsible for working out solutions to problems he creates. This was a problem that Eric could handle with God's help.

Vern

Derek's friend, Vern Cole, with whom he had committed many offenses in the past, came from a family that has had conflict as long as he can remember. When Vern was four, his father left for work one day and never came back. He waited half the night for his father to come home and learned the next day that his mother had called the police accusing her husband of beating her. So his dad left. A few days later, his mother's boyfriend, Mr. Mather, moved in. Although they have never married, he has fathered one of Mrs. Cole's children.

Vern's father moved in with another woman in Oklahoma. He never remarried either, but still lives with her. They have three children. Mr. and Mrs. Cole have never gotten a divorce.

Vern's father and mother are alcoholics. When Vern was six, he started drinking whatever liquor his mother had in her bottle. By the time he was twelve, he was a steady drinker.

In junior high, Vern met Derek; they started hanging around together. Vern was fourteen when they stole the BB guns from the auto supply store. It was a regular habit to shoot out car lights and windows. If they felt mean, they hit people through open car windows as they drove by at night. They snatched old ladies' purses and loved to indulge in "window-peeking"—watching married couples make love.

120

Vern was sixteen the next time he broke into the auto supply store. That same year he was caught breaking into a home. After a weekend in jail he was put on probation. Probation was a small deterrent to illegally entering stores. He continued the same pattern until he was caught running out of a school with his pockets full of coins freshly heisted from a pop machine. He got two months in jail.

Vern knew the Ralstons and through Loren's help he became a Christian. Loren got Vern out of jail and into a foster home, because of his poor home situation and constant conflict with his mother.

For four months Vern stayed out of trouble. But then he returned to his real home and all the old problems ignited anew. Fights commenced at school. Stealing started again. He broke into store after store. He became a heavy drinker. Finally things caught up with him.

Vern, Scott Bower and another friend stole a 1962 Chevy. Because their reputation was too well-known in Wichita, they split to an adjoining community where it was safer to knock off a store. Their mistake was in picking a rural town that was not overly fond of blacks coming around after dark. The police were attracted to them like iron to a magnet.

Vern and his cohorts feared the police had a missing car report so they decided to outrun the cops. To their dismay, their "hot" car would not go over seventy miles per hour, eliminating any hope of ditching the cops. As the police closed in, Vern remembered a creek where he used to go fishing. Since he knew the area well he figured they could lose the cops in the creek and walk back to Wichita.

Vern was not driving, so he told Scott to make a turn at the next corner. Scott was so scared he kept saying, "I'm going to stop. I'm going to stop."

Vern yelled at the top of his voice, "Nigga, if you stop you ain't ever moving again."

Scott did not stop. He did not make the turn at the next corner either. They were caught.

Guilty of car theft, Vern spent the next three months in jail. His sentence should have been one to five years at the State Reformatory, but the judge let him off with these sobering words, "If you ever get caught again, you will get the original sentence plus whatever the sentence for the next crime should be."

Those stern words made a profound impact on Vern. He wasn't involved in stealing for a while. He returned to high school as a senior, preparing to graduate in a semester. It was not long before he was in a fight in the school hallway and was suspended for the year.

After suspension from school, Vern went to Job Corps in Ogden, Utah to train in heavy equipment and cooking. But he was involved in six fights in the first two months. His reputation grew daily. One day he jumped on his heavy-equipment instructor and whipped him. He was almost dismissed, but they decided to allow him to remain.

During the summer of 1972, our staff met Vern. Because of his likable personality we never realized how bad his background or reputation was.

In December, Vern returned to Wichita. Al said it would be good for him to live in our house. In January he moved in, attended the Bible studies and started to mature in his Christian life. As Vern observed the radical change Christ produced in the lives of his close friends like George, Charlie and Derek, he turned areas of his own life over to the Lord.

George and Charlie took Vern everywhere they went and demonstrated a real love. Vern's change came slowly,

122

Vern Cole, Frank Anderson and children

a day-by-day growth. He memorized verses and before long, he was the key person in checking to be sure that everyone had done his Scripture memorization and Bible study. He was our Christian "enforcer."

In a chapel service at Tabor College, Vern gave his testimony, telling the student body how God made him a new creature in Christ. An incident three days earlier graphically portrayed the new creature Vern is.

He was walking across the street in a crosswalk when a "white dude" drove extremely close, almost sideswiping him. When Vern turned around the dude flipped him the finger. A year ago the old Vern would have beaten the driver senseless. But the new Vern responded, "That's O.K. brother. Jesus loves you anyway."

Vern has a strong desire to see his family find Christ and often asks Christians to pray for them. He is frustrated by glib Christian solutions that "God would bring his father and mother back together again." He has five brothers and sisters by his real parents, one brother by Mr. Mather and his mother, and three brothers and sisters by his father and the woman with whom he is living. Is it any wonder Vern can't understand how God could ever patch up his home situation?

It wasn't all roses for Vern after he accepted Christ. Sin still tempted him—old habits are hard to overcome. During the meat crisis Vern stole $200 worth of meat from a butcher while he lived at our "Christian house."

A few days later I conducted a training session for our summer staff which Vern attended. In explaining 1 John 1:9 I used the following illustration "If I stole some meat from Al's refrigerator and as I walked out the door, shut my eyes and confessed to God, 'I stole Al's meat,' I wouldn't be forgiven. When the Bible says to 'confess our sins' other things are implied. First, I need to ask God to convict me, make me feel sorry for the thing I did wrong (I knew it was wrong because the Bible said 'Do not steal'). When I was convicted then I would have to ask God to forgive me, tell Al what I did, explain that God had forgiven me (He promises to if we are truly sorry), and ask for Al's forgiveness. Then I must return the meat."

At this time I was ignorant about Vern's recent caper. After the meeting, Vern approached me: "You don't love me anymore, do you, Keith?"

"Why do you ask?" I questioned.

"You found out about the meat I stole" he confessed.

As God's Spirit convicted Vern he had the rare experience of practically applying 1 John 1:9. Vern realized that theft was not the way to support our ministry, so he confessed his sins and asked God to forgive him. He then told the butcher he stole the meat.

The butcher stood stone still, amazed that a thief would admit his crime, and wondering whether this was cause for joy or fear.

Vern continued, "I am a Christian now and God convicted me of stealing. I want to work all summer and pay you back. Would $20 a week be reasonable?"

The butcher gladly took the payments for ten weeks.

The forgiveness of God and the butcher increased Vern's faith in the Bible. Vern is on our full time Los Angeles staff today, leading youth clubs in Watts and telling dudes about Jesus.

Discipleship

Discipleship is a key ministry of World Impact. It takes place when a mature Christian invests his life in a new babe in the Lord, helping the new believer become strong

125

in his Christian life, so that he can evangelize and train others.

Discipleship is a scriptural mandate: "Go therefore and make disciples" (Matt. 28:19, *NASB*). We see discipleship occurring in our Wichita ministry. Al meets daily with the older Christians, who in turn meet with the younger ones. For every individual we are discipling now, we see five more who are ready to be discipled. We realize the importance of solidly grounding these first few in the Word even while holding an eager expectation of reaching more. We see a solid core of black Christians developing spiritual leadership that will spearhead revival in urban Wichita.

EIGHT

CASTLES IN OMAHA

In 1967, Charlie Wells was twenty-five years old, had a wife and two children, and was working for the telephone company. He didn't know God and wasn't seeking to know Him. No one had challenged him to become a Christian.

One night he had a hard time sleeping. His brain raced through the pros and cons of seeking a promotion into management with the company. This would mean moving his family and changing his life-style. His mind was also burdened with the deeper problems of the purpose of life and his place in the world.

Suddenly a voice spoke to him, "I want you to work for me." That was all. Charlie was wide awake. There was no doubt that it was the voice of God.

Was it a real voice? Was it audible or just in his head? Charlie says today, "Yes, it was a real voice. I was awake tossing around on the bed when I heard it." His immediate reaction was a strong awareness of his unworthiness and evil. The voice spoke again, "I will forgive you. Ask me." Charlie simply replied, "Forgive me and use me if you can." Then he saw himself preaching God's Word.

Charlie is still amazed that this happened to him. Slightly embarrassed, he admits that God spoke to him directly. "It makes me out to be more of a mystic than I am," he says modestly.

He woke up in the morning with an unquenchable thirst to know more about God. "I didn't understand what I had done until I began reading the Bible. There I found other men asking forgiveness and then following Christ. I knew this was a turning point in my life. In the next few months I read the New Testament through several times. With no one helping me or teaching me, I began to understand who God was, and what salvation, sin and forgiveness were all about."

Charlie worked for the telephone company for two more years to pay off his debts. In 1969 he enrolled in Grace Bible Institute in Omaha.

In May, 1971, I spoke in a chapel service at Grace Bible Institute, challenging the student body with the need in urban Omaha. This midwestern city was plagued with racial tension. A white police officer was shot in predominantly black North Omaha producing a white-black cleavage. A gospel of reconciliation needed to be lived and preached.

128

It was determined that Grace Bible Institute students would start to lead inner-city youth clubs the following school year. One hundred college students pledged themselves to minister weekly as club leaders for urban youth.

Charlie Wells was one of the volunteers. He was anxious to get started in something that would really count for God. His dedication and ability impressed me and I invited Charlie to direct our youth club program in Omaha. He accepted.

After two training sessions the students started youth clubs. Crafts and Bible story curriculum were sent from Los Angeles. We had no recreation equipment, and no money. Charlie bought ten good quality footballs for $75.00 and donated them to World Impact (what else could he do?). During the school year they were all stolen.

The club attendance increased week after week. Students became more excited, building relationships, and continuing to learn. Scores of youngsters and adults committed their lives to Christ.

Eight-year-old Linda faithfully attended club at the Logan Fontenelle Housing Project. She accepted Christ as her Saviour on October 2, 1971, the fifth week of youth clubs. But in November she was absent for three weeks in a row. Linda had become sick and died before the end of November. She was a Christian for five weeks before she met her Lord. Her club leader put it this way, "It's all worthwhile. One soul in heaven because of World Impact. Praise only the Lord!"

As boys and girls, men and women became Christians, they needed their own copies of God's Word. Initially, we gave Bibles away. Since many youngsters came to club with candy or pop, we realized that they could at least subsidize the cost of a Bible. If they invest money in God's

129

Charlie Wells

Word it means more to them. One club leader related, "I handed one of the Christian girls in my club a Bible and asked if she could pay a dollar for it. She said she'd pay twenty-five cents a week for four weeks. Three other girls gave me a dollar right then."

Not All Are Successes

The first contact with boys is made by starting a football game in the center of a housing project. During one of the games Roy Hall met Eddie. After the game the conversation turned from football to Eddie and his life at the housing project. Eddie asked about God, sin and heaven. Roy shared God's plan of salvation with Eddie and showed him what the Bible says about receiving Christ. Eddie invited Christ to forgive his sins and control his life.

Roy wrote Eddie during the week to encourage him in his decision. The next Saturday Roy, back at the project, noticed that Eddie didn't say much during the game. After the game Roy didn't approach Eddie, but Eddie came to Roy and said, "I told Andre, a friend from school, about my decision. Andre came to club today because he wants to accept Christ, too." Roy led Andre to Christ.

Not every relationship blossoms into a Disney-like ending. While Roy presented the plan of salvation to three boys, Morgan sat outside the group listening. When Roy finished he asked Morgan what he thought of Christ.

Morgan said, "I would like to have my sins forgiven and know I am going to heaven."

Morgan professed to trust Christ as his Saviour. A few weeks later Roy contacted Morgan to see how his relationship with Christ was maturing, but Morgan didn't want to talk to Roy. He pretended not to remember making a decision to follow Christ. A year later, Morgan's picture was in the newspaper. He had murdered a security guard at a department store.

Growing Up Too Fast

An Omaha club leader remarked in his weekly report, "I wonder how they (inner-city children) can take so much growing up so fast." The comment is profound. Ghetto youngsters are forced to mature almost from infancy. Many never enjoy the luxury of childhood. They suffer from the instability of splintered families—the labyrinth of half- or step-brothers and sisters, fostered by hit-and-miss fathers. They fight for identity in one-parent households whose residents number in double figures. They are responsible for caring for younger family members before they are ten. They wander and roam streets without parents' permission or knowledge. No one cares. They're weaned on the common acceptance that promiscuity is a valid norm.

Overindulgence in liquor parallels an illicit flow of drugs. Manhood is measured by fighting. Hurt feelings can't be coped with except through violence. Stealing is fine—if you don't get caught. Lack of self-confidence and achievement leads to hating others and, worst of all, hating self.

It is true. Many cannot take growing up so fast.

Don't Tell Me What to Do

Marshall Tate, a black man, is a twenty-year veteran of the armed forces, a probation officer in Omaha, and the pastor of a small church in the ghetto. I met Marshall in the Omaha courts where he was on trial for resisting arrest.

Marshall's teen-age daughters were walking along the sidewalk in front of their North Omaha home when a

132

squad car drove up beside them. The officers started asking them a bevy of questions. They were afraid since black-police relationships were strained. Two days before there was a bombing aimed at the police. Questioning by an officer usually signaled that an arrest was soon to follow and the girls were frightened. They ran into the house looking for their father.

Marshall appeared at the front door and asked the officers in. One yelled, "Get out here. Don't tell me what to do!"

A bit indignant, Marshall repeated his invitation for the officers to come inside and talk the matter over reasonably. They refused again. Marshall wrote down their badge numbers so he could report their unjust treatment.

One officer retorted, "I'm taking you in for causing a public disturbance and disturbing the peace." When the officer tried to handcuff him, Marshall's left arm would not reach behind his back. While in the service, Marshall was hit by a jeep in Okinawa which resulted in his having limited use of his left arm. It was impossible for him to reach behind his back. The officer interpreted this as resistance and since no one else on the street witnessed the event, Marshall was charged with disorderly conduct and booked. In spite of the service records confirming Marshall's physical condition, the court found him guilty.

Sherwood Houses

With the youth clubs' success we prayed for a house in North Omaha where a live-in ministry could be conducted. Marshall introduced me to Dean Drickey. He owned two castle-like structures in North Omaha, half a mile from the housing projects where scores of youth had committed their lives to Christ. It was a perfect location for follow-up and out-reach.

The two houses were in dire need of repair, as are most of them, but they were beautiful to us. Each building had four separate apartment units. Each unit had a kitchen, two or three bedrooms, a bath, dining room and living room.

Mr. Drickey originally asked for more than twenty thousand dollars for the two houses. When we talked to him, sharing our ministry, he came down to eight thousand for both. He wanted a five-hundred-dollar down payment before the end of the year with $75.00 monthly payments beginning the following June.

I wanted to be sure the houses were God's will and not ours. Late that evening Marshall Tate, Charlie Wells and I drove to these two houses on Sherwood Street. We didn't have a key so we broke in through one of the front windows that bordered on the porch and crawled into the big vacant building. Marshall and I were excited about the potential of these castle-like structures; Charlie wasn't so enthusiastic. Plaster was falling off the walls, the floors were warped, the roof leaked, the plumbing was faulty. But overall it looked great to me. We walked upstairs over garbage and trash to a center room. There we bowed for prayer.

I asked God to dampen a fleece I was about to fling out. If He wanted us to have these buildings, I asked Him to give us $1,000 within ten days, from people who had never given to us before.

Marshall was all for the acquisition. Charlie kept saying things like, "Keith, it'll cost a fortune to fix up. Who's going to do the work? Who'll pay for it all?"

Later, Charlie confessed, "While you were asking God

to show us that He wanted us to have the building, I was praying that He'd show us that He didn't want us to have it." Charlie wanted a house in good condition, all ready to move in. This house didn't fit his dream.

That dark night, I left the Sherwood houses in peace, knowing it was entirely in God's hands.

The next morning I walked out of the chapel at Grace Bible Institute, sharing with a professor the prayer we had prayed. I told him of the excitement I had about the matter being completely up to God and of my anticipation in waiting to see how God would answer.

Mr. Enns, a carpenter working close by, overheard our conversation. He grabbed my arm and told me he was interested and would donate the first fifty dollars. "Praise the Lord," I replied. He invited me to visit him and his wife that evening and pick up the check.

Mr. Enns was a retired gentleman from Fresno, California, who was donating six months of his time to Grace Bible Institute to do carpentry work. He and his wife wanted to see the buildings.

Upon arrival at the Sherwood Street houses, Mr. Enns walked around and marveled at the spacious rooms. Then, as a carpenter would, he went to the basement and inspected the joists, beams and general structure. His verdict was positive. The only thing he said was, "Are you sure they only want eight thousand dollars for both buildings?" I assured him that this was true.

As we drove back to their apartment, the Enns were very quiet. When we got there, I got out of the car to talk to their son while Mr. and Mrs. Enns stayed in the car to talk and pray for a few moments. Then Mr. Enns said, "My wife and I have prayed . . . and decided not to give you the first fifty dollars." As he paused, I felt my heart sink. I was sure these people were going to be the beginning of a miracle. Then he added, "Instead, we're going to give you the first five hundred."

Praise the Lord. I was so thrilled I had to call Charlie. He said, "Since God provided five hundred dollars tonight, I'll donate the next fifty."

I left Omaha for Los Angeles with $550 in my pocket. Six days after we put out our fleece, God moved again, and sent us a $450 check for the live-in ministry in Omaha. Exactly one thousand dollars! We didn't receive another penny for three months toward that property. God answered us precisely in six days with not one penny more, not one penny less. We bought the houses.

Deserted

Three single men moved into the Sherwood Houses in the fall of 1971. They visited their neighbors often and shared Christ. In January of 1972 Omaha was experiencing a cold spell with sub-zero temperatures and high winds. Two teen-age boys in the neighborhood arrived home from school one afternoon to find their house locked. Their parents had deserted them and fled to St. Louis. With no money, shelter or food their only recourse was to take to the streets. As soon as we knew of their dilemma, we invited them to live at Sherwood. Food, clothing and beds were provided. In time they committed their lives to Christ.

Where Is God, Anyway?

As Charlie and Agnes began preparing themselves emotionally for their move into the Sherwood Houses, Agnes discovered she was pregnant with their third child.

How does a young wife feel about moving into the

ghetto? Agnes claims it was exciting for her. Since becoming a Christian, she had a conviction that when God calls a man into the ministry, He calls his family also. "As long as Charles is where God wants him," she says, "that is the safest place for me and the children. I can't say that I had any apprehensions at all about moving into the ghetto because I felt that the atmosphere of our home would be the same wherever we were."

Charlie was taking twelve and a half hours of classes each week at Grace Bible Institute, studying, working thirty hours a week in a secular job and directing the youth club ministry. Soon he was being treated for high blood pressure; but he was determined to move into the house by summer.

By springtime little had been done to the physical structure of the house. We had no money for repairs and no volunteer labor. We were recruiting a staff to direct the summer work and live in the houses.

In April I told three Omaha churches that we needed volunteer workers to help remodel the two buildings—in four weeks the summer staff was scheduled to move in. Charlie organized the volunteers.

Inside the houses tons of drywall panels were stacked in piles on the floor. None was on the walls yet. Charlie and six men from local churches started nailing on drywall that Saturday, April 8. That same day they completed two-thirds of the unit to be used as a women's dorm. That was the beginning of seven hundred hours of labor for Charlie alone on the houses.

Since few laymen returned to help on the renovation, Charlie put most of his time into manual labor instead of outreach. "I was forced into a deeper faith in God," Agnes relates, "when Charlie came home one night and said he had decided to quit his part-time job so he could spend more time fixing up the house. I knew God would take care of us somehow. I also knew that with the baby on the way I couldn't do as much to help Charlie as I would have liked."

They had no income through May and June. During this time they survived on some savings and small gifts from friends.

"I was so busy I didn't have time to worry about our income," Charlie remembers, "and I guess that was an advantage. My full load at school was heavy. The youth club ministry was growing like crazy which created more work for me to do there."

I was in Omaha one May afternoon and dropped in to see Charlie. He stood in the midst of falling plaster; the walls and ceilings were full of holes. Water dripped from leaking pipes on the already-warped floor boards, increasing the smell of mildew.

"What will we do, Keith?" was his plea. "We can't possibly finish in time. Look at this mess. And it isn't only what you see and smell, the electric wiring is so faulty it's dangerous and the whole plumbing system is a nightmare."

"Haven't you been getting any help?"

"Very little, and that's the most discouraging part. Here I am, excited about the prospects of the ministry and so few people share my vision. I get the feeling that few Christians care."

I wondered how to answer him. It *did* look like an impossible task. "The only thing that comes to my mind, Charlie, is to try to see the job in units small enough to be worth attacking."

"I know you're right," he said, "but sometimes I get so

138

Sherwood House renovation

completely fed up that I drive over to our nice apartment. I feel like crying all the way across the city. But I can't."

Agnes encouraged Charlie by telling him how great the house would be when it was complete. She visualized the finished product and made scale drawings of the house on paper and sketched in where her furniture should be. She wanted to restore some of the fireplaces, but they were being used to vent the furnace and could not be opened. "I didn't even get to keep one mantel," she said.

Finally, the Omaha inspection department scribbled a long list of items that didn't meet approval. The main problem was an outside staircase which they classified as a fire escape. The wooden stairs were rotten and some steps were missing. Two Christian carpenters donated four successive Saturdays and rebuilt the steps. A Christian plumbing contractor donated all the needed plumbing fixtures, supplies and labor. A Christian electrical contractor gave a 20-percent discount on his work. A pastor laid brick for us.

By May 22 we had moved our staff girls into an upstairs apartment and christened it the Girls' Dorm. They slept on the floor on mattresses. The walls were drywalled, but that's all. The floors were a mess. For four days the girls "rolled up" their beds, stuck them in the closet and joined the renovation work.

Charlie moved his family into their apartment on June 24. It was a mess! The drywall was nailed on the walls and ceilings. The electrical work had been done and the kitchen cabinets were in place. The plumbing was "finished" in the upstairs bathroom. But when the water was turned on, water poured down through the Wells' kitchen ceiling from an undetected broken water pipe. Charlie was furious. What else could happen? Where was

Painting walls of Sherwood House

God anyway? Didn't He know what was going on?

About eight o'clock that night, Charlie went to buy a pry-bar. He knew he had to tear out part of the floor upstairs to get to the broken water pipe. He went to a discount store—no pry-bar. So he bought a screwdriver. He went to another merchant, no pry-bar. So he bought another screwdriver. He said, "I'm going to keep buying screwdrivers until I find a pry-bar." At the third store he found a pry-bar. He was up until 1:00 A.M. tearing up the floor so the plumber could get to the pipes.

"Why, God? Why? I'd rather have a nice little congregation somewhere, and a parsonage," Charlie sighed.

141

So moving day was rather discouraging with their possessions piled in the middle of the room and covered with plastic sheets to protect them from the onslaught of filth, dust and paint. The apartment stayed this way for seven weeks waiting for the drywall finishers.

Once Agnes spilled some sauce on the kitchen floor. She started to clean it up, but, it wasn't worth the effort. The sauce was simply assimilated by the rest of the dirt.

There were two bathrooms in their apartment, one upstairs and one down. They used the upstairs toilet, but had to wash their hands and take their baths downstairs. They couldn't use their washing machine for two months. Agnes couldn't use the kitchen sink for washing dishes, so she washed them in the bathtub.

"There was no use fretting about it because it wouldn't have helped a bit." She relates, "I had a large-sized foot tub, larger than a dishpan, which I filled with soapy water. I put it in the tub alongside a dishpan filled with rinse water and a plastic dish drainer. I sorted the dishes and stacked them in separate piles on the kitchen counter.

"I'd put the glasses and silver into the foot tub, wash them and put them into the dish pan to rinse. Then back to the kitchen for the plates, move the silver and glassware into the drainer, carry them back to the kitchen, dry them, put them away and back to the tub to continue the process. Our bathtub is the kind that sits on four legs, so with the outer edge of the tub under my arms, there was room under the edge for my ever-growing tummy.

"When the nightly ordeal was over, I'd dump the dishwater and rinse water into the tub and down the drain, rinse the pots and pans and clean the tub. I couldn't leave them in the tub until the next day because we all had to take baths.

142

"I often wondered, as I knelt there beside that tub washing dishes, what plans God had for us in Sherwood House. Why were we going through such extreme hard times? Was it to make us strong? Or was it to test our willingness to serve Him no matter what?"

Growing Pains

The summer staff was involved in daily youth clubs, Adult Bible Studies and rapping with teen-agers. Sharing Christ was preeminent, but they also did a lot of cleaning, painting, hanging curtains and moving furniture.

As the staff returned from youth club one afternoon, they saw a woman slumped beside a car with two children bending over her. The staff drove the semiconscious woman to a nearby medical center and took her inside in a wheelchair.

The doctor told the staff that the mother was in a diabetic coma from lack of insulin and lack of food. After she felt better the staff paid the hospital bill and took her to Sherwood House where she slept. The children told the staff that the family had come from Ogallala, Nebraska for the boy's checkup; he had muscular dystrophy.

After the staff fed and prayed for the family the boy invited Christ into his life. Soon the family was on their way with expressions of love and appreciation.

Later a bi-racial couple was referred to Charlie by a local social service agency. Carmen was white and Sam was black. They had just arrived from New York with their two children, hoping to find work and a place to live. We gave them supper and a bed for the night.

The next morning four of our girls couldn't find their purses. They told Charlie about the theft just before Carmen and Sam were about to leave. Charlie asked them to

Charlie Wells training Grace Bible students

wait for the police to arrive. We later discovered that they were innocent.

Charlie relates, "It was a bad scene. They charged us with discrimination and the woman became very emotional. This was our first big mistake at Sherwood House. We were learning and this was one of the growing pains. There are no easy answers. How do you handle such sensitive situations? When a crime occurs, do you call the police or not? Learning is often painful, both for us and for others. We apologized, but the scar on the relationship was permanently fixed. We had communicated distrust!"

The girls' dorm and the Wells' apartment were finished one week before classes reconvened at Grace Bible Institute.

"It was a funny feeling," Agnes says, "crawling around on the floor with my tummy nearly dragging as I cleaned up after the drywall finishers. Then I got the woodwork ready for Charlie to paint. I started in one doorway armed with a wet rag and a putty knife. I'd scrape and wipe, following the woodwork all around the room. Charlie followed me with the paint brush. We were racing against time; the time for the baby to come and the time for Charles to return to school. I had to huff and puff to keep ahead of Charles. Sometimes I wondered what the doctor would think if he knew what I was doing between visits.

"The most exciting part came after we got the painting done and the rugs laid. The floors were such a mess and when we got the rug laid in the utility room upstairs, the new home of my washer and dryer, everyone ooh'd and ah'd. It was great having one clean room in the house. Everything was finished in our apartment two weeks before the baby came."

145

I'm the One That's Colored

A major concern of any white couple moving into a predominantly black area is the effect of the environment and ministry on their children. John the Wells' oldest, remarked, "I'm glad we moved here. Now I see that everyone is really just alike, no matter what his color."

The children had a few adjustments to make after they started attending school. Patti, a first grader, was the only white youngster in her class. John was one of three in his fifth grade. For two or three weeks Johnny was pushed, punched, called names and systematically excluded from most athletic events.

Charlie warned him, "Don't fight. Sometimes it will be hard to ignore a nasty remark or a punch, but fighting only gets you hurt and solves nothing."

When Johnny was shoved out of a school line, the boy who was the most antagonistic toward John asked him why he didn't hit the other boy back. John replied, "Oh, I don't know, I kind of like the guy." This was the ice-breaker. From then on Johnny was accepted by most of the boys.

I asked John how he liked school. He said it was rough at first because his dad wouldn't let him fight back, but he was beginning to feel that pacifism was the best policy. "Just today on the way home," he said, "a boy kicked Patti in the rear. I wanted to slug the guy but when I turned around and said, 'Hey, why'd you do that?' the kid pulled a knife and said, 'What about it?'

"It's amazing how God helps you remember what's right and wrong," he added, "I suddenly remembered I wasn't supposed to fight."

Agnes prayed a lot when the kids started school. She

realized it was an adjustment they would have to make on their own. They knew how a Christian should act and she encouraged them in that respect. She left the rest in God's hands. She hurt as much as John did when the other boys wouldn't let him play football, a game he loves and is good at. But before long he was able to pick any position he wanted to play on the team.

Agnes hurt when Patti came home from school and told about being pinched, kicked and picked on. But what an insight this child has. "Now I know what it feels like to be black," she told her mother, "because in my class I'm the only one that's colored."

Does Agnes worry about the children? She answers emphatically, "No! I don't worry because God will take care of them," and then she adds, "I do worry about whether I've helped them grow in the right way so they are prepared to meet and overcome life's problems and temptations. That's my responsibility and I don't want to fail there. My family is my mission field, no matter where we live."

In the sixth grade Johnny was given a "commendable service award" for unselfishly serving his school. The award was signed by his teacher and principal, but it was voted to him by his predominantly black classmates. Last year he was voted to serve on the student council. Next year, Johnny goes to Horace Mann Jr. High. Charlie says, "I'm a little apprehensive because of the problems with drugs and violence, but we'll take it as it comes. This school has a good faculty and John has high aspirations for running for student body president. He's working on poster and handbill ideas already for his massive campaign."

Hatred and Apology

In the spring of 1972, Charlie approached Donna Willis, a Grace Bible Institute student, believing that God wanted her to head up the girls' work at Sherwood House. She wasn't as positive as Charlie about God's will for her life when he first approached her. "But," she says, "since Charlie was convinced that I would come to World Impact, I naturally started praying about it, and God showed me it was His will."

In July the "Plus One" singing group from Portland, Oregon, was on tour. In Omaha they sang at youth clubs, parks and special concerts. After their program at the Logan-Fontenelle Park, there was a rock and bottle throwing war among some of the project teen-agers. Rocks, bottles and bricks flew through the air as Charlie and Donna helped the "Plus One" pack their equipment. One of the neighborhood boys they brought to the concert got slugged and was bleeding at the mouth. Charlie had his two children with him and was concerned for their safety as well as that of innocent bystanders. It was so dark you couldn't see the flying objects, just hear them whistling by.

In the midst of this they met Billie, a tough teen-age girl who acted and dressed like a boy. She was involved in the "war" and made no bones about it. They invited her to drop by Sherwood House any time. It became obvious to Donna as she asked and answered questions that Billie knew the Bible. Billie began coming to club.

In September Billie came to Sherwood House for the first time. She talked quite a while. Then she either visited the house or talked over the phone to Donna every day, sometimes more than once.

Donna met Billie's family at a party—everyone was

smoking weed with a pipe and drinking wine. Billie was a heavy user of drugs: LSD, pills and weed and they messed up her mind. She stole cars, tape decks and bikes. She led a small gang in vandalism, stealing and beating people up. They would steal anything that wasn't bolted down. She fired at her sister and others with a .38 revolver.

Billie loves fire. She set fire to her own house and to the caboose of a train. Everyone in North Omaha has heard of Billie.

She took a great interest in Donna and offered to wash her car, move boxes or do anything that pleased Donna. When Billie became tough, Donna stood up to her and refused to be pushed around.

Billie claimed to be a Christian but her life bore little testimony to the Christ within her. After frequent and stormy discussions about this she prayed again, and said, "This time I really mean it." Her life seemed to change. She showed a strong desire to please God—and Donna.

Donna spent hours with Billie; took her to the movies, shopping, driving, studied the the Bible and prayed with her. Whenever Billie got out of line, Donna brought her back to the Bible with, "But, God says. . . ." Often, then, Billie lashed out at Donna.

Once when Donna corrected her, Billie became furious. She yelled, screamed and refused to leave the apartment, challenging Donna to drag her out. She slugged Donna on the head and in the ribs. Charlie heard the commotion, came into the house and sat down between Donna and Billie. He asked Donna, who was in tears, what had happened. As Donna related the events, Billie admitted they were true. Billie was angry because Donna had spent time with a male friend.

Charlie said, "Do you think that's the way a Christian

should act?" Billie quieted down, bowed her head in shame and said, "No, it isn't. I'm sorry, Donna, I won't do that again."

Less than month later, in a supposedly playful mood, Billie tried to jab a girl with a stick who was curled up on the ground. Donna stopped her by taking away the stick. Billie grabbed it, it broke, and Donna dropped it.

Billie screamed, "Pick up my stick!"

Donna didn't move a muscle.

"Pick it up, do you hear me?" Billie's face was contorted in anger. She suddenly moved toward Donna and slugged her in the jaw. Donna staggered, but stood up straight and looked her in the eyes. Billie finally said, "Oh, Donna, I'm so sorry, I didn't mean to do that. Please forgive me, I'll never do it again. Never!"

Again, Charlie rushed to Donna's aid and asked her if Billie had hit her.

"Yes, but it's O.K., Charlie, it's O.K."

Sometimes Billie wanted to live for God, sometimes she wanted to show Donna how bad she could be. Most of the time she wanted to run her own life without God.

Billie saw Christian love displayed by Donna and the other staff members. She couldn't understand how they could love her even when she was so mean. She said, "No one else ever loved me like this."

In December, Billie was put in jail for assaulting an officer with a bow and arrow when the officer tried to intervene in a family dispute. Billie and her sister were fighting when someone called the police. When a squad car appeared, Billie phoned some friends, got the bow and arrow and took off after the group of police who were trying to be peacemakers.

Donna received permission to visit Billie at the youth

150

center where whe was confined. After the hearing a few days later, Donna took Billie home.

Billie continued to threaten Donna on many occasions. Once she came at her with a hunting knife. Donna talked Billie into surrendering it. Anger raged when Donna refused to return to Billie this unique "relic of her ministry."

Billie likes basketball, track and roller skating. She boxes well and gets paid for it. She claims to know judo and karate.

Four of the six children in her family are living. Only Billie and one brother have the same father. Her mother married only once. The family isn't poor. They live better than the World Impact staff! Billie has nice clothes, but usually wears jeans with one of two or three tops. She is illiterate, unable to discern words like "what," "there" or "is." She's been kicked out of four schools for fighting with students or the teachers.

Rumors around North Omaha were that Billie had been part of a gang rape at least twice. She bought her girl "friends" expensive gifts, watches and rings. She gave Donna a silver band ring worth twenty-five dollars.

One time Donna and Billie went for a sight-seeing ride around North Omaha. They ended up in a secluded area where there was little traffic and Billie asked Donna to stop the car so they could talk. Soon she became aggressive and wanted to kiss Donna. Donna wouldn't fight with Billie for fear she would reject Christ.

Donna wasn't dumb but she was definitely naive. But what can you expect? The problem is one for which we cannot prepare our staff in advance of a real-life incident. How many white, middle-class, small-town Christian girls have had experience with lesbians? It was 1:00 A.M.

before Donna finally talked Billie out of her intentions and returned home. Donna was an emotional wreck. Our staff was confused, frustrated and felt a bit helpless.

A few days later Billie visited Donna again. She wanted a ride home from the Girls' House, and, since Donna had to pick up the members of her junior high girls' club she said, "I'll take you straight home, Billie, but nowhere else." It was 8:30 P.M.

They no sooner left the Sherwood House than Billie moved close to Donna. She tried to force Donna to drive to a secluded place again, threatening to beat her up if she didn't. She kept saying, "I'm not a lesbian, Donna, I'm a man. And to prove it I'll rape you."

Donna drove into a large grocery store parking lot a few blocks from home and drove right up to the door of the market. She jumped out of the car, leaving the keys behind, and ran into the store begging the security guard for help. He said, "I can't do anything to help you," so Donna phoned Charlie.

"Billie tried to assault me again and she's taken off with my car keys. All the Sherwood House keys are attached."

Charlie arrived at the market to take Donna home. A block away Charlie spotted Billie. He slammed on the brakes, jumped out of the car and started chasing her. Billie ran into the next street. Charlie ran after, right down the middle of the street, dodging oncoming traffic.

Around the corner and down a block he caught her. He grabbed the back of her jean pocket, turned her around and slammed her down over the trunk of a parked car. He frisked her but found no car keys. "I passed them on to a friend," she said.

Meanwhile a car pulled up with a man and woman in it. The man shouted, "Hey, what's goin' on?" Charlie looked

152